CALL US
WHAT WE
CARRY

AMANDA GORMAN

POEMS

CALL US WHAT WE CARRY

VIKING

VIKING
An imprint of Penguin Random House LLC, New York

First published in the United States of America by Viking,
an imprint of Penguin Random House LLC, 2021

Visit us online at penguinrandomhouse.com.

Library of Congress Cataloging-in-Publication Data is available.

Book printed in the United States of America

ISBN 9780593465066

1   3   5   7   9   10   8   6   4   2

WOR

Design by Amanda Gorman and Jim Hoover   Text set in Garamond Premier Acta Book

For all of us
both hurting & healing
who choose to
carry on

Contents

History and elegy are akin. The word "history" comes from an ancient Greek verb ἱστωρειν meaning "to ask." One who asks about things—about their dimensions, weight, location, moods, names, holiness, smell—is an historian. But the asking is not idle. It is when you are asking about something that you realize you yourself have survived it, and so you must carry it, or fashion it into a thing that carries itself.

—ANNE CARSON

SHIP'S MANIFEST

Allegedly the worst is behind us.
Still, we crouch before the lip of tomorrow,
Halting like a headless hant in our own house,
Waiting to remember exactly
What it is we're supposed to be doing.

& what exactly are we supposed to be doing?
Penning a letter to the world as a daughter of it.
We are writing with vanishing meaning,
Our words water dragging down a windshield.
The poet's diagnosis is that what we have lived
Has already warped itself into a fever dream,
The contours of its shape stripped from the murky mind.

To be accountable we must render an account:
Not what was said, but what was meant.
Not the fact, but what was felt.
What was known, even while unnamed.
Our greatest test will be

Our testimony.

This book is a message in a bottle.

This book is a letter.

This book does not let up.

This book is awake.

This book is a wake.

For what is a record but a reckoning?

The capsule captured?

A repository,

An ark articulated?

& the poet, the preserver

Of ghosts & gains,

Our demons & dreams,

Our haunts & hopes.

Here's to the preservation

Of a light so terrible.

REQUIEM

Now let us issue from the darkness of solitude.

—Virginia Woolf, *The Waves*

PLEASE

ensure you maintain [   ] yourself & others & [   ] face

[   ] all [   ] [[   ] people [   ] in [   ] time.

ARBORESCENT I

We are
     Arborescent—
What goes
     Unseen
Is at the very
     Root of ourselves.
Distance can
     Distort our deepest
Sense
     Of who
We are,
     Leave us
Warped
     & wasted
As winter's
     Wind. We will
Not walk
     From what
We've borne.
     We would

Keep it
　　　　For a while,
Sit silent &
　　　　Swinging on its branches
Like a child
　　　　Refusing to come
Home.　We would
　　　　Keep,
We would
　　　　Weep,
Knowing how
　　　　We would
Again
　　　　Give up
Our world
　　　　For this one.

AT FIRST

There were no words for what we witnessed.
When we talked to each other,
Our sentences were stilted
& stalled as a telegram.
Hope we are doing well/
As we can be/
> *In all these times/*
>> *Unprecedented & unpresidented.*

When asking how others were faring,
We did not expect an honest or full response.
What words can answer how we're remaining alive?
We became paid professionals of pain,
Specialists in suffering,
Aces of the ache,
Masters of the moan.
March shuddered into a year,
Sloshing with millions of lonely,
An overcrowded solitude.
We pray there will never be such a
Precise & peopled hurt as this.

We began to lose words
As trees forget their leaves in fall.
The language we spoke
Had no place for *excited,*
Eager, laughter, joy,
Friend, get together.
The phrases that remained
Were their own violence:
That was sicckk!

Ha! we're dead.
We are deceased.

To try is to take a stab,
To take a shot.
We want to find who made us
A slaughterhouse,
A rhetoric that works in red.
We teach children:
Leave a mark on the world.
What leads a man to shoot up
Souls but the desire to mark

Up the globe?
To scar it & thus make it his.
His intention to be remembered,
Even if for a ragged wreckage.
Kids, unmark this place.
Leave it nothing
Like the one we left behind.

Sorry for the long text;
There are no small words in the mouth.
We find the rhetoric of reunion
By letting love reclaim our tongues,
The tip of the teeth.
Our hearts have always
Been in our throats.

FUGUE

Don't get us wrong.
We do pound for what has passed,
But more so all that we passed by—
Unthanking, unknowing,
When what we had was ours.

There was another gap that choked us:
The simple gift of farewell.
Goodbye, by which we say to another—
Thanks for offering your life into mine.
By *Goodbye*, we truly mean:
Let us be able to say hello again.

This is edgeless doubt:
Every cough seemed catastrophe,
Every proximate person a potential peril.
We mapped each sneeze & sniffle,
Certain the virus we had run away from
Was now running through us.

We slept the days down.
We wept the year away,
Frayed & afraid.

Perhaps that is what it means
To breathe & die in this flesh.
Forgive us,
For we have walked
This before.

History flickered in
& out of our vision,
A movie our eyelids
Staggered through.

We added a thousand false steps
To our walk tracker today
Because every step we've taken
Has required more than we had to give.

In such eternal nature,
We spent days as the walking dead,

Dreading disease & disaster.
We cowered, bone-shriveled
As a laurel in drought, our throats
Made of frantic workings,
Feet falling over themselves
Like famished fawns.
We awaited horrors,
Building up leviathans before they arose.
We could not pull our heads
From the raucous deep.
Anxiety is a living body,
Poised beside us like a shadow.
It is the last creature standing,
The only beast who loves us
Enough to stay.

We were already thousands
Of deaths into the year.
Every time we fell heart-first into the news,
                    Head-first, dread-first,
Our bodies tight & tensed with *what now?*
Yet who has the courage to inquire *what if?*

What hope shall we shelter
Within us like a secret,
        Second smile,
                Private & pure.

Sorry if we're way less friendly—*
We had COVID tryna end things.
Even now handshakes & hugs are like gifts,
Something we are shocked to grant, be granted.
& so, we forage for anything
That feels like this:
The click in our lung that ties us to strangers,
How when among those we care for most
We shift with instinct,
Like the flash of a school of fish.
Our regard for one another
        Not tumored,
                Just transformed.

By *Hello*, we mean:
Let us not say goodbye again.
There is someone we would die for.
Feel that fierce, unshifting truth,
That braced & ready sacrifice.
That's what love does:
It makes a fact faced beyond fear.
We have lost too much to lose.
We lean against each other again,
The way water bleeds into itself.
This glassed hour, paused,
Bursts like a loaded star,
Belonging always to us.
What more must we believe in.

* In fact, levels of social trust have been in a steep decline in the United States. See
David Brooks. Strikingly, a 2021 study suggests that the descendants of the survivors of
the 1918 influenza epidemic experienced lowered social trust. See Arnstein Aassve et al.

SCHOOL'S OUT

The announcement
Swung blunt as an axe-blow:
All students were to leave
Campus as soon as possible.

We think we cried,
Our brains bleached blank.
We were already trying to forget
What we would live.
What we would give.

* * *

Beware the ides of March.
We recognized that something ran
Rampant as a rumor
Among our ranks.
Cases bleeding closer,
Like spillage in a napkin.

There is nothing more worrisome
Than a titan who believes itself
Separate from the world.

* * *

Graduation day.
We don't need a gown.
We don't need a stage.
We are walking beside our ancestors,
Their drums roar for us,
Their feet stomp at our life.
There is power in being robbed
& still choosing to dance.

THERE'S NO
POWER LIKE HOME

We were sick of home,
Home sick.
That mask around our ear
Hung itself into the year.
Once we stepped into our home,
We found ourselves gasping, tear-
ing it off like a bandage,
Like something that gauzed
The great gape of our mouth.
Even faceless, a smile can still
Scale up our cheeks,
Bone by bone,
Our eyes crinkling
Delicately as rice paper
At some equally fragile beauty—
The warbling blues of a dog,
A squirrel venturing close,
The lilt of a beloved's joke.
Our mask is no veil, but a view.
What are we, if not what we see in another.

WHAT WE DID IN THE TIME BEING

❑ We strove to be new-muscled & green,
❑ To exercise,
❑ To express,
❑ To stay home,
❑ To stay sane,
❑ To render our ovens beating with breads,
❑ Our phones shining with excuses for parties.

We grasped our loved ones
By the slash of a screen,
Felt ourselves Zoombies,
Faces trapped in a prison of a prism.
The petty zoo[m] as it were.
& what could we have done differently?
We only have one way to not die.

It will be a blessing if our children
Never fully grasp what
It took to come to this.

❑ Grant them this poem
    If they do forget it.
❑ If they do, forget it.

SURVIVING

These words need not be red for our blood to run through
     them.
When tragedy threatens to end us, we are flooded by what
     is felt;

Our faces fluctuating, warped like an acre passing
Seasons. Perhaps the years are plotted & planned

Just like seeds in a fresh-plowed field.
When we dream, we act only with instinct.

We might not be fully sure of all that we are.
& yet we have endured all that we were.

Even now we're shuddering:
The revelation aching.

It didn't have to be this way.
In fact, it did not have to be.

The gone were/are no threshold,
No stepstone beneath our feet.

Even as they did not die
For us, we shall move for them.

We shall only learn when we let this loss,
Like us, sing on & on.

THE SHALLOWS

Touch-deficient &
Light-starved we were,
Like an inverted flame,
Eating any warmth down to its studs.
The deepest despair is ravenous,
It takes & takes & takes,
A stomach never satisfied.
This is not hyperbole.
All that is gorgeous & good & decent
Is no luxury, not when its void
Brings us to the wide wharf of war.

Even as we stand stone-still,
It's with the entirety of what we've lost
Sweeping through us like a ghost.

What we have lived
Remains indecipherable.

& yet we remain.

& still, we write.

& so, we write.

Watch us move above the fog

Like a promontory at dusk.

Shall this leave us bitter?

      Or better?

Grieve.

Then choose.

& SO

It is easy to harp,
Harder to hope.

This truth, like the white-blown sky,
Can only be felt in its entirety or not at all.
The glorious was not made to be piecemeal.
Despite being drenched with dread,
This dark girl still dreams.
We smile like a sun that is never shunted.

Grief, when it goes, does so softly,
Like the exit of that breath
We just realized we clutched.

Since the world is round,
There is no way to walk away
From each other, for even then
We are coming back together.

Some distances, if allowed to grow,
Are merely the greatest proximities.

CUT

There is no simple way to hurt.
The real damage is dammed, disrupted.
:Inaudible:
We must change
This ending in every way.

* * *

Disease is physiological death,
Loneliness is a social one,
Where the old We collapses like a lung.

* * *

Some days, we just need a place
Where we can bleed in peace.
Our only word for this is
Poem.

* * *

There is no right way to say
How we have missed one another.
Some traumas flood past the body,

An ache unbordered by bone.
When we shift toward a kindred soul,
It is with the cut of all our lives.
Perhaps pain is like a name,
Made to sing just for you.

* * *

We issue an apology
From our warbling palms:
      We are still hurt,
But for now, we no longer hurt
          One another.
There is no meek way to mend.
You must ruin us carefully.

GOOD GRIEF

The origin of the word *trauma*
Is not just "wound," but "piercing" or "turning,"
As blades do when finding home.
Grief commands its own grammar,
Structured by intimacy & imagination.
We often say:
We are beside ourselves with grief.
We can't even imagine.
This means anguish can call us to envision
More than what we believed was carriable
Or even survivable.
This is to say, there does exist
A good grief.

The hurt is how we know
We are alive & awake;
It clears us for all the exquisite,
Excruciating enormities to come.

We are pierced new by the turning
Forward.

All that is grave need
Not be a burden, an anguish.
Call it, instead, an anchor,
Grief grounding us in its sea.
Despair exits us the same way it enters—
Turning through the mouth.
Even now conviction works
Strange magic on our tongues.
We are built up again
By what we
Build/find/see/say/remember/know.
What we carry means we survive,
It is what survives us.
We have survived us.
Where once we were alone,
Now we are beside ourselves.
Where once we were barbed & brutal as blades,
Now we can only imagine.

WHAT A
PIECE OF WRECK
IS MAN

History is a ship forever setting sail.
On either shore: mountains of men,
Oceans of bone, an engine whose teeth
shred all that is not our name.

—Tracy K. Smith, "Ghazal"

ESSEX I

The *Essex* was an American whaling ship that was attacked by a sperm whale in 1820. Of the twenty crewmen, only eight survived, only eight were rescued after being stranded at sea for three months. The tragedy inspired Herman Melville's *Moby-*

Take tragedy, write a book. Look. Only when we're drowning do we understand how fierce our feet c an kick. We were mar, marred & moaning, thick sea. How much more wreck do we have within us. Wherever we look, there's a body des troyed. We were told never to use I when writing, because eliminating this voice makes arguments le gitimate. But we realize there is nothing that convin ces like the self does—our life, our body & its beating, proving its own jagged point. Tell us what is more pow erful than the unerased. Those men spent months, lost on waves, seeing no faces but their own, bleached by a se a of burns. Wait long enough & boys can become barbed as beasts, beards dripping down their chests like scarves. Does what survives, what is salvaged, need to be so savage? Is this the sea we rise from, not more animal, but more human? Haggard. Hobbled. Heart-strung. Yes. But human. & human. In other wor ds, we become what we hunt, as we inevitably begin to think like our prey. The slain fueled the lamps of a world latched to nights, our whole century brightened by blood. When that whale slaugh tered their ship, there was no doubt that hatred could live hosted in a creature. Whaling is like going to war, we may not return from the illegible wreckage. Drifting by now on shaking, small boats, the

Dick. At the time, whales were killed for blubber, which was utilized in oil lamps as well as other commodities.

I'm not telling you a story so much as a shipwreck—the pieces floating, finally legible.   —Ocean Vuong, *On Earth We're Briefly Gorgeous*

stranded crewmen turned away from the promise of land, dreading
cannibals, those red fables of the foreign. That one decision stre
tched out their horror the length of a raging ocean. Were we
any different, any less rent, rapt & lost. Loss is undecipher
able. Can you even be rescued if you've been ruined.
We can see them now, after the fever of months,
at the tail end of their blue nightmares,
the flesh of friends flush against
their teeth. They had eaten 7
of their own men. We
become what we flee
& what we fear.
Who can pay
the price of
light. We may
be wrong.
We are wrong often.
But we refuse to believe
that the only way we learn
is by whip & woe, the dart of disaster.
Contrary to popular belief, it's not easy for us
to lie. Even the body has tells, even our blood runs toward
truth. We are born right, trusting,   unlimited, with all that we love
never banished. Look—our   palms open but unemptied,
just like a blooming thing. We're   walking forward, also harboring
just this   one life.

CALL US

Grant us this day
Bruising the make of us.

At times over half of our bodies
Are not our own,

Our persons made vessel
For non-human cells.

To them we are
A boat of a being,

Essential.
A country,

A continent,
A planet.

A human
Microbiome is all the writhing forms on

& inside this body
Drafted under our life.

We are not me—
We are we.

Call us
What we carry.

ANOTHER NAUTICAL

All water has a perfect memory and is forever trying to get
back to where it was.   —Toni Morrison

The English noun suffix -*ship* is unrelated to the vessel.

Rather it means "quality, condition, skill, office."

The suffix's origin is from the Old English *scieppan*, signifying
"to shape, create, form, destine."

Add -*ship* to the end of a word & it transforms its meaning.

Relation	→ship
Leader	→ship
Kin	→ship
Hard	→ship

Add -*ship* to the end of a world & it transforms our meaning.

This book, like a ship, is meant to be lived in.
Are we not the animals, two by two,
Heavy hearted & hoofed, horned,
Marching into the ark of our lives.
We, the mammals marked to flood
This day throbbing into tomorrow.

* * *

To ship, in colloquial terms, means to imagine or place as a pair,
to push two persons or things together, whereby we ship them.
It is a shortened, verbed version of *relationship*, to dream of love
where there was blankness.

    Relationship   → ship

Sometimes the extract is not an erasure,
But an expansion.
It is not a cut, but a culmination.
Not a gash, but a growth.

Life has taken the suffix -*ship*, made it a verb,
       Taken a sound
             & given it momentum.

That's what only words can do—
Prod us toward something new
& in doing so, move us closer → together.

Perhaps our relationships are the very make of us,
For fellowship is both our nature & our necessity.
We are formed primarily by what we imagine.

There truly is a unity
That requires no "they"
For us to be threatened by.
This is the very definition of love.
We've never had to hate a human
To hug another, never had to be fearful
To be fond of the hearts beating out to us.

This whole sea-less wreck,
We have sought
Not yellow land
But our fellow man,
The shores mapped
Only by one another.

Willed across wine-dark woes,
We arrive at ourselves.

* * *

Hope is the soft bird
We send across the sea
To see if this earth is still home.
We ask you honestly:
Is it?

* * *

We, like the water, forget nothing,
Forgo everything.
Words, also like the water,
Are a type of washing.
Through them we cleanse ourselves
Of what we are not.
That is to say, words
Are how we are moored & unmarred.
Let us rouse & roar
Like the ancient beasts we are.

IN THE DEEP

We swam through the news
Like a ship bucking at sea.
For a year our television
Was a lighthouse, blinking
Only in warning & never in warmth.
We felt ourselves things bred in the night,
Hibernating from our own humanity.
Grief made ropes of our arms.
This whole time, what we craved most
Was only all that we have ever loved.
* * *
The hours roved listless as a bike
Drunk without its handles.

Until.
When.
Back to normal,
We repeat, an incantation
To summon the Before.
* * *

We mourn the past
More than we miss it.
We revere the regular more
Than we remember it honestly.

Don't we recognize
All the ways
Normal can
S p u tt e r
&
Die.

* * *

Yes, nostalgia has its purposes—
Transport from the spectered,
The jobs never coming back,
The mothers' primal screams,
Our children's minds shuttered from school,
The funerals without families,
Weddings in waiting,
The births in isolation.
Let no one again
Have to begin, love, or end, alone.

* * *

The earth is a magic act;
Each second something beautiful
On its stage vanishes,
As if merely going home.
We have no word
For becoming a ghost or a memory.
To be a member of this place
Is to remember its place,
Its longitude of longing.
This elegy, naturally, is insufficient.
Say it plain.
Call us who we left behind.

* * *

It's not what was done that will haunt us,
But what was withheld,
What was kept out & kept away.
The hand clenched tightly
With every black blow.
We cannot fathom all these phantoms.
But do not fear our ghosts.
           Learn from them.

* * *

Slowly as the sea,
We found the stubborn devotion to say:
Where we can we shall hope.
We found it in a million delicacies
Of enormity—
An infant's full-chested chortle,
July glassing our skin,
Music blurring a summered street.
How when we're among friends
Our laughter can stomp
Up from nothing.
Through this hole punched in the roof
We can see a stitch of sky.
Our wounds, too, are our windows.
Through them we watch the world.

* * *

We prayed for a miracle.
What we got was a mirror.
Watch as, without movement,
We gather together.
What have we understood? *Nothing. Everything.*

What are we doing?

Listening.

It took us losing ourselves
To see we require no kingdom
But this kinship.
It is the nightmare, never
The dream, that shocks us awake.

LIGHTHOUSE

Homo sum, humani nihil a me alienum puto.

—Terence

We have never met
& yet we have still lost sight of each other,
Two lighthouses quavering in fog.
We could not hold ourselves.

This year was no year.
When next generations ask, we will say
It went something like this:
The empty, creaking playgrounds,
Bodies laid straight as celery stalks,
The imprint of warmth, holidays,
Gatherings & people, gone to rust
In our acrid skull.
The moments wavered unscheduled,
Planless, not plotless. Time col   lap   sed
Into no m   ore than   a shape
That we felt for numbly

(& tell us: what is the hour
But a rotation by which we mark our grief).
Whole months swept by, fast but dragging,
Like a damp void trapped in the rearview.
Our souls, solitary & solemn.

By then, our fear was old & exact,
Worn-in & stiff as a hand-me-down.
When has horror not been our heirloom.

* * *

The heart, chambered by grief.
The mind, assimilated to suffering.
Nevertheless, we walked from that pale plane,
Though we were free to remain.
Hope is no silent harbor, no haven still.
It is the roaring thing that tugs us away
From the very shores we clutch.

Though we have never met,
We have sensed the other all along,
Quiet & wandering, wide-lit
With the urge to move forward.
No human is a stranger to us.

COMPASS

This year the size of a sea
Sick to its stomach.
Like a page, we are only legible
When opened to one another.
For what is a book
If not foremost a body,
Waiting & wanting—
Yearning to be whole,
Full of itself. This book is full
Of ourselves. The past is one
Passionate déjà vu,
One scene already seen.
In history's form, we find our own faces,
Recognizable but unremembered,
Familiar yet forgotten.
Please.
Do not ask us who we are.
The hardest part of grief
Is giving it a name.

The pain pulls us apart,
Like lips about to speak.
Without language nothing can live
At all, let alone
Beyond itself.

Lost as we feel, there is no better
Compass than compassion.
We find ourselves not by being
The most seen, but the most seeing.
We watch a toddler
Freewheel through warm grass,
Not fleeing, just running, the way rivers do,
For it is in their unfettered nature.
We smile, our whole face cleared
By that single dazzling thing.
How could we not be altered.

HEPHAESTUS

Pay attention.
Having fallen
In this era of error,
We're re-raised among wreckage.
What happened to us,
We asked. A true inquiry.
As if we're simply the affected,
The recipient, to which
Such rambling trauma was sent.
As if we did not give the very cry
To which our bows were bent.

We labor equally
When we fall as when we rise.
Always remember that
What happened to us
Happened through us.

We wonder how close
Can we come to light
Before we shut our eyes.

How long can we stand the dark
Before we become more than our shadows.

Pay attention.
Concern is the debt
We always owed each other.

* * *

This is not an allegory.
Descend into ourselves,
Like a fruit caught by its own branch.
That clear plunge is the beginning
Of what we ought to become.

* * *

Say our feet miss a step on a stair—

Shock zagging hard up our veins—

—Even as our foot forgives the ground.
The blood jaggedly striking in our veins
Reminding ourselves we are perishable
But prevailing, living & livid.
   Sometimes

         The fall

         Just makes

            Us

            More

               Ourselves.

EVERY DAY WE ARE LEARNING

Every day we are learning
How to live with essence, not ease.
How to move with haste, never hate.
How to leave this pain that is beyond us
Behind us.
Just like a skill or any art,
We cannot possess hope without practicing it.
It is the most fundamental craft we demand of ourselves.

CORDAGE, or ATONEMENT

[Hensleigh Wedgwood, *A Dictionary of English Etymology*, 1859]

Call us fish-meal.
We are no prophet.
We are no profit.
Our whole year swallowed,
As if by a massive maw.
What else could stomach
Our hearts, huge with hurt,
Everyone & everything hell
-shocked, as a sea bait-
ing its breath, its time.
As if to hold its whole self.

Lasting meant being separate
Together, proximate in our distance.
To be a part of the living,
We had to be apart from it,
      Alive but alone.
It was death by survival.

* * *

    The word *atone* comes
From the Middle English meshing
Of *at* & *on(e)*, literally "at one," "in harmony."
By the second half of the seventeenth century, *atone* meant:

"to reconcile, and thence to suffer the pains of whatever
sacrifice is necessary to bring about a reconciliation."

There swims our one hope,
Unintelligible in its massiveness,
Like a finback dragging itself under.
& harrowed as we are,
We're still standing
Gold as a beach,
Despite all augury, proof
That the meek shall repaireth the earth.

* * *

Call us Odd'Sis,
Wily as these miles of bloodshed.
Our gods owe men omens.
        Answers, we mean.
We hide a battalion in the body

Of this poem, wild as a wolf in the woods.

Strength is separate from survival.
What endures isn't always what escapes
& what is withered can still withstand.
We watch men mend their amens,
Words flapping against their hands.
Poetry is its own prayer,
The closest words come to will.

Come the tenth year in this battle,
We will no longer allow shadows
A free tenantry within us.
We would leap out of this night
Down-rushing on our head.
Often we cannot change
Without someone in us dying.

* * *

Call us an exodus,
Plagued ten times over,
For all we see is red.
Intentional language, like a poem,

Is to separate our waters like a gash,
To find the sea also grieving & giving
Enough to be walked through.

* * *

No.
We are the whale,
With a heart so huge
It can't help but wail.
We can't help but help.
If given the choice, we would not be
Among the Chosen,
But amidst the Changed.

Unity is its own devout work,
The word we work in,
That leaves us devastated to be delivered.

The future isn't attained.
It is atoned, until
It is at one with history,
Until home is more than memory,

Until we can hold near
Who we hold dear.

What a marvelous wreck are we.
We press out of our cold
& separate crouching.
Like a vine sprung overnight,
We were reaching & wretched
Upon this mortal soil
& even so we are undiminished.
If just for this newborn day,
Let us take back our lives.

EARTH EYES

so knowing,
what is known?
that we carry our baggage
in our cupped hands
when we burst through
the waters of our mother.
—Lucille Clifton, "far memory"

LUCENT

What would we seem, stripped down
Like a wintered tree.
Glossy scabs, tight-raised skin,
These can look silver in certain moonlights.
In other words,
Our scars are the brightest
Parts of us.

* * *

The crescent moon,
The night's lucent lesion.
We are felled oaks beneath it,
Branches full of empty.
Look closer.
What we share is more
Than what we've shed.

* * *

& what we share is the bark, the bones.
Paleontologists, from one fossilized femur,
Can dream up a species,
Make believe a body
Where there was none.
Our remnants are revelation,
Our requiem as raptus.

When we bend into dirt
We're truth preserved
Without our skin.

* * *

Lumen means both the cavity
Of an organ, literally an opening,
& a unit of luminous flux,
Literally, a measurement of how lit
The source is. Illuminate us.
That is, we, too,
Are this bodied unit of flare,
The gap for lux to breach.

* * *

Sorry, must've been the light
Playing tricks on us, we say,
Knuckling our eyelids.
But perhaps it is we who make
Falsities of luminescence—
Our shadows playing tricks on stars.
Every time their gazes tug down,
They think us monsters, then men,
Predators, then persons again,
Beasts, then beings,
Horrors & then humans.
Of all the stars the most beautiful
Is nothing more than a monster,
Just as starved & stranded as we are.

LIFE

Life is not what is promised,
But what is sought.
These bones, not what is found,
But what we've fought.
Our truth, not what we said,
But what we thought.
Our lesson, all we have taken
& all we have brought.

ALARUM

We're writing as the daughter of a / dying world / as its new-faced alert. / In math, the slash / also called the solidus / means division, divided by. / We were divided / from each other, person / person. / Some griefs, like rivers, are uncross / able. They are not to be waded across / but walked beside. Our loss / colossal & blossomed / is never lost on us. Love the earth / like we've failed it. To put it plain / we have shipwrecked the earth / soiled the soil / & run the ground aground. / Listen. We are the loud toll / on this planet. / Our future needs us / alarmed. Man is a myth / in the making. / What is now dust will not return, / not the beloveds / nor their breath, / nor the sugar-crumbling glaciers, / nor the crows chewing / on their own soured song, / nor all the species / slashed / down / in one smogged swoop. / Extinction is a chorus / of quiet punching / that same note. What can never be brought back / can still be brought forth / in memory / in mouth / in mind. To say it plain is to tell / only half / of the story.

EARTH EYES

What have we done.
Currently our jaw is clamped down,
our shoulders nailed to the ears, bones braced for
brutal battle. By *Think of the next generation* we mean:
Every day this very ground spoils beneath us, for we are bringing
to all the ends of the Earth the end of all the Earth. Please believe us
when we say we, too, ache to imagine something new. Reparation lies
not in the land we own, but the very land we owe, the soil & toil we thieved
in from the start. Nothing is a grander summitry than this: water, drinkable;
our air, breathable; birds, built & blurred on a breeze; trees heaving huge sighs
into the heavens; our children, giggling & gilded in grass. Earnest for the first
time, we must earn this turned Earth back. Now we are begged to save it. We
screech with kids who must fix the world because braving it is no longer
enough. *The youth will save us*, they say. But even that is its own release.
Our short lives now aimed at the oily-headed monsters that reared
their teeth before we even gave our first wet croak. Generations
of the past order, be our recruits, not our rescues. Oh,
how we want our parents red & restless, as
wild & dying for a difference as
we are.

ARBORESCENT II

Like trees,
        We're always
Scoping out
        Heat,
Not with
        Our eyes
But the blur
        Of our bodies,
The celestial
        Stitched inside us.
Slant upward,
        For there
Are ways
        To sit &
Let joy find
        This injury,
Even
        As we
Let loss

Wash around
Our head
        Like
A low
        Sound.
We grasp
        At the very best
Of each
        Other
 & begin.

CAPTIVE

The animals flooded our streets
Demanding answers or food,
Here to take back
What was theirs.
We were swept up by an unsung
Need for nature,
For the sky slack with blue,
The studded stirring of stars.
That June we kicked off our shoes,
Feet sticky with summer & sat
On somebody else's lawn,
If just to let grass steam up
Our toes. We're still in that green,
Shuttering the discs of our eyes,
The bark of us swaying
Not by any breeze imaginable.

[Animals in captivity will demonstrate what is termed
stereotypic behavior: repetitive & unvarying actions

that have neither goal nor function. Some examples
of stereotypic behavior include incessant pacing, over-
grooming, rocking, kicking, excessive sleeping & self-
mutilation.]

Our (re)collection
Is gray & stormed.
Isolation is its own climate.
Six months & we still could not grasp
What we were losing every minute.
We stalked ourselves for days in our own house,
Absolutely abulic, incessantly incensed.
We chewed our nails to the knuckles,
Ground our teeth to stardust,
Flipped unpolluted memories
Over in our mind like a penny
Rubbed faceless for good luck.
We walk daily with the dying
Of the earth. The hopes hoarded
Behind our throat, an extinction.
What, exactly, is meant by "normal"?
What, exactly, is meant?

[Stereotypies are demonstrated in many animals, including
elephants, horses, polar bears, macaques & humans.
Because stereotypic behavior is not seen in the wild, it is
considered a strong indicator of poor psychological health
in the caged organism. Thus, stereotypies are termed
abnormal (or, rather, the captive environment is the true
abnormality). Smaller cages can exacerbate stereotypies.
To be captive, then, is to be rendered a trope of oneself.]

The same sapiens, we flooded our streets
Demanding answers & change.
To love is to be liable
To ourselves & each other.
Our need for nature
Is our need for origins,
The green tangled place
Where we are of least consequence
& yet still matter as much as anything.
We count each organ-ordered
Throb that makes us this upright mammal.
Among ants, at times even the queen
Must carry & bury her dead.

We cannot tally all we would give
Just to be this unbeaten heart.

[Locked down, the animal may perform the behavior in the
same way over & over, at the same time over & over, in the
same place, over & over, with the same results. What we're
describing is insanity. Or 2020.]

Perhaps there's a day with no tattered terrain
Of terror, only an ether strung into
Blue. The beauty of the planet,
When we remember to look,
Stuns us blank as babes.
To care is how we vow
That we are here,
That we are.
It is how we break
Free.

PAN

Pandemic, meaning all people.
Pandemonium, meaning
all demon. Pandora,
meaning all-gifted.
Pan, meaning god
of nature. All people
have meaning, are all-
demon, all-gifted. It is in
our divine nature. We now
appreciate that Pandora's box was a jar
left ajar, a pithos (to tell the mistranslation,
then, is to risk being remembered by its fiction),
meaning a storage container for grain, oil, wheat
& even the dead. We all need places to lay down
our grief. Where else to put it. That vessel held
all plague, all pain & all hope. Don't panic.
Instead, turn to a companion. What are we
if not the curiosity to open the coffins
we carry, who are we if not
all the things we let loose.

MEMORIA

It can take billions of years for light to reach us
through the galaxies, which is to say, History is
ever arriving.

—Don Mee Choi, *DMZ Colony*

MEMORIAL

When we tell a story,

We are living

Memory.

In ancient Greece, the Muses, the dainty-footed daughters of Memory, were thought to inspire artists. It isn't knowing, but remembering, that makes us create. This would explain why so much great art arises from trauma, nostalgia, or testimony.

But why alliteration?
Why the pulsing percussion, the string of syllables?
It is the poet who pounds the past back into you.

The poet transcends "telling" or "performing" a story & instead remembers it, touches, tastes, traps its vastness.

Only now can Memory, previously marooned, find safe harbor within us.
Feel all these tales crushing our famished mouth.

PRE-MEMORY

Marianne Hirsch posits that the children of Holocaust survivors grow up with memories of their parents' trauma; that is to say, they can remember ordeals that they did not experience personally. Hirsch calls this postmemory. Seo-Young Chu discusses what she calls postmemory han, han being a Korean conception of collective grief. Postmemory han, then, is the han passed on to Korean Americans from previous generations. As Chu writes: "Postmemory han is a paradox: the experience being remembered is at once virtual and real, secondhand and familiar, long ago and present." The whiplike echo of Jim Crow, too, passes through Black bodies, even before birth.

* * *

Trauma is like a season, deep & dependable, a force we board our windows against.
Even when it passes, it will wail its wild way back to our porch.

We destroy everything good just so it will not shame us.
How easy it is to both leave & love this place.

* * *

In this manner, collective memory need not be experienced firsthand to be remembered. Grief, healing, hope are not dependent on the first person & more often than not are recalled through many persons.

Similarly, in Spanish, like in many languages, the verb's conjugation often takes the place of a pronoun. *Llevo* means "I carry." The pronoun *yo* (meaning "I") is made unnecessary. The "I" is assumed, not absent. *Lleva*, for example, in itself can mean she/he/it/you carries or carry. Something similar, if not exponential, happens with postmemory. Postmemory is not the solo but the choir, a loyal we, to be not above others, but among them. The trauma becomes: I/she/he/you/they/we remember. I/she/he/you/they/we were there.

* * *

Even beside each other, it was in terror.
Who else has mistaken pain for proximity.

Don't believe a word from our mouths.
We'll say anything to keep from drowning.

* * *

We posit that pre-memory is the phenomenon in which we remember that which we are still experiencing. It is how we understand a current reality as a collective memory, even as said reality continues to unfold. The recollections do not belong to a single person, nor do they have a determinate chronological end. The assertion becomes: I/she/he/you/they/we know. I/she/he/you/they/we are here.

* * *

Poke the scar until it speaks.
This is how every memory starts.

We droop our head in two,
Into an echo struck long before.

* * *

There are some of us who, when experiencing a tragedy or comedy in our lives, already think: *How will this be told to another? Can it be told? How can we possibly begin the story of what has happened to us?*

Pre-memory defines who we are as a people. Will we forget, erase, censor, distort the experience as we live it, so that it cannot be fully remembered? Or will we ask, carry, keep, share, listen, truth-tell, so it need not be fully relived?

It is the moral difference between collective amnesia & collective remembrance.

Storytelling is the way that unarticulated memory becomes art, becomes artifact, becomes fact, becomes felt again, becomes free. Empires have been raised & razed on much less. There is nothing so agonizing, or so dangerous, as memory unexpressed, unexplored, unexplained & unexploded. Grief is the grenade that always goes off.

* * *

A smile around here is like a sudden star, undead & loaded. To live only to die is to be doomed but redeemable.

All we know so far is we are so far
From what we know.

WHO WE GONNA CALL

What is writing but the preservation of ghosts?

—Cameron Awkward-Rich,

"Essay on the Appearance of Ghosts"

We rouse ghosts,
Primarily, for answers.
Meaning we seek
Ghosts for their memory
& fear them for it just the same.
Our country, a land of shades.
Yet there are no wraiths but us.
If we are to summon
Anyone or anything,
Let it be our tender selves.

* * *

Like ghosts, we have too much
To say. We will make do,
Even if in a graveyard.
We, like this place,
Are haunted & hungry.
The past is where we pull home,
Our forms once again fluent
In all things bright.

WHEN

We forget this immensity, it will still be ours, for we wrote
such mysteries down: we did the thing others dared not.
We collected all the dazzling & dangerous & dreamed
aches, scrapped them, though we did not yet have words by
which to map them.

Someone will remember us, this, even if in another time,
even if by any other name.

We wrap our arms around ourselves, as if we can possibly
hold the whole of who we are within us—everything that
makes us this unearthly speck we are. Perhaps tomorrow
cannot wait to be today.

In this one life, we, like our joy, are fleeting but certain,
abstract & absolute, ghosts who glow & glow.

VALE OF THE
SHADOW OF DEATH
or
EXTRA! EXTRA!
READ ALL ABOUT IT!

Goodbye! (at the close of a letter); (in taking leave
of the dead); . . . to be worth; (with genitive or ablative
of price or value); to mean, signify; *parum valent Graeci
verbo* the Greeks have no precise word for this (but we
call it 'night') —.

—From Anne Carson's definition of *vale* in *Nox*

We promise to write the truth.

Stay with us till the end.

This is how a word blooms into a virus & then into a body & then that body into bodies.

The "Spanish" influenza did *not* originate in Spain. In fact, the first recorded case was in the United States—in Kansas on March 9, 1918 (bewareth March). But because Spain was neutral in World War I, it did not censor reports of the disease to the public.

To tell the truth, then, is to risk being remembered by its fiction.

Countless countries laid blame to one another. What the US called the Spanish influenza, Spain called the French flu, or the Naples Soldier. What Germans dubbed the Russian Pest, the Russians called the Chinese flu.

It's said that ignorance is bliss. Ignorance is this: a vine that sneaks up a tree, killing not by poison, but by blocking out its light.

———————

The 1882 Chinese Exclusion Act blocked all Chinese laborers from immigrating to the US. It was the first federal law in the United States to differentiate between "legal" & "illegal" immigration. It was signed after generations of stereotyping Chinese immigrants as the carriers of cholera & smallpox.

Again, words matter(ed).

The first step to scapegoating a whole people is to delegitimize their value—to call them a host to nothing but horror.

Something in us repents every time a new friend doesn't tell us their given name, preempting our tongue to lay a violence toward that too.

Heritage is passed not in direct recollection but through indirect retelling. Those who follow will not remember this hour, but this hour will surely follow them.

———————

Follow along.

This discord is so ancient it makes fossils of us all, a history no longer entirely our own &

yet only ours, never understood.

In Spain, *vale* (pronounced like *ballet*) carries many meanings: "okay," "understood," "good," "all right." The verb *valer* means "to cost, to be worth," much like the English word *value*, yet in Spain *vale* thrives under a different resonance.

Although called "Asiatic cholera," the disease thrived in Europe. Smallpox had originally been brought to the Americas not by Asians, but by European invaders, contributing to the deaths of millions of Native peoples.

Sometimes, we must call our monster out from under the bed to see he/she/it carries our face.

———————————————

Some will hate our words because they burst from a face like ours.

When the 1918 flu epidemic reached Chicago, John Dill Robertson, the city's commissioner of public health, blamed the African Americans who had fled the South's Jim Crow oppression for Northern cities. In the same lake-hugged city where our grandmother & mother would be born, on July 8, 1918, the *Chicago Daily Tribune* ran the headline: "Half a Million Darkies from Dixie Swarm to the North to Better Themselves."

Stay. We promise, we are going somewhere, okay?

Vale?

The *Tribune* reporter Henry M. Hyde wrote that Black people "are compelled to live crowded in dark and insanitary rooms; they are surrounded by constant temptations in the way of wide-open saloons and other worse resorts."

The oppressor will always say the oppressed want their over-crowded cage, cozy & comforting as it is; the master will claim that the slaves' chains were understood, good, all right, okay— that is to say, not chains at all.

A racial insult renders us a mammal, albeit less free.

In short, a slur is a sound that beasts us.

———————————————

This will never sound good, understood, all right:
In 1900 Surgeon General Walter Wyman described the bubonic plague as an "Oriental disease, peculiar to rice eaters."

As if we are what we eat & not also who we cheat, what we tweet.

He was dead.

What we mean is he was dead

Wrong.

We can only fully understand language by what doesn't survive it.

In this way, ignorance is a sound that beats us—blue, black, yellow, red, a wretch of a rainbow. In Spanish, the definite article *the* is used far more frequently. It's not blue, it's *the* blue, *el azul*. The black, *el negro*. Not history, *the* history. As if there froth many pasts & we must be clear on which one we are forgiving, if any.

Our country, which we do not forsake for being un-great, that we should find by being good.

Goodness is how we move our words into something new: a kind of grace. In Spanish, the word for *value* is the same as for *bravery*: *valor.* Courage must cost us something, or else it is worth nothing at all.

Who more shall pay & for what. If we understand this at all, say *vale.*

This act speaks for itself, as if to say: we know all it means to lift our head from our hands, to exit this shadow that we call night.

We have walked the skyless depths it cost for us just to be all right.

This feeling might be pain, poetry, or both. But at least it is no lie.

Ignorance isn't bliss. Ignorance is to miss: to block ourselves from seeing sky.

We swear to write the whole truth, as at the close of a letter. Farewell to all that makes us less than seeing or seen. Brave, upright beasts that we are, slide out of the curve of a long-lived blue. Its promise is the only articulate truth between us. The sky is colossal, undenied & yet understood. Maybe no one can pay the price of light. We yoke any warmth for all it's worth.

BACK TO THE PAST

At times even blessings will bleed us.

There are some who lost their lives
& those who were lost from ours,

Who we might now reenter,
All our someones summoned softly.

The closest we get to time travel
Is our fears softening,

Our hurts unclenching,
As we become more akin

To kin, as we return
To who we were

Before we actually were
Anything or anyone—

That is, when we were born unhating
& unhindered, howling wetly

With everything we could yet become.
To travel back in time is to remember

When all we knew of ourselves was love.

ATONEMENT

But I am hunting for something—anything—
to give me some bearing, since I am,
metaphorically speaking, at sea, having cut
myself off from the comfort and predictability
of my own language—my own meaning.

—M. NourbeSe Philip, *Zong!*

ERASURE

Several of the following are erasure poems, meaning
they're documents with their pieces plucked out, just as
some will call this the gone year, the long year, the glove
year, the unlove year. The key to constructive—& not
destructive—erasure is to create an extension instead of
an extract. It's not erasure, but expansion, whereby we
seek the underwriting, the undercurrent beneath the
watered surface of the words. It is to keep the words from
drowning. Hereby the pen looks to enhance, evoke,
explore, expose the bodies, the truth, the voices that have
always existed but have been exiled from history & the
imagination. In this case, we erase to find.

The Letters

In a letter I received from you two weeks ago
I noticed a comma in the middle of a phrase.
It changed the meaning—did you intend this?
One stroke and you've consumed my waking days.

—Lin-Manuel Miranda, *Hamilton*

CONDOLENCE

Our scourge was to tell
The death of Cecilia—

Impossible

This plague attacked
                    It was brought here
It spread rapidly

Stopped regular activities
                    Devoted itself absolutely

We lost comparatively everything possible

The sick was never one someone

We want to feel

                    This sickness

Spared neither expense nor time nor trouble.
Altogether we could be done

This disease upon the country
Was worse here than elsewhere

It was not due

Now that the plague resumed
Our work we have now

Trusting body we are*

---

* Letter of condolence from Superintendent of the Yakama Indian Agency,
Washington, October 29, 1918. Bureau of Indian Affairs.

LETTER FROM A NURSE

Everybody has to die
We consider ourselves lucky
Believe us
We were there & yet we intended staying,
Home a whole string of things we can't begin to name
Oh!
The first that died sure unnerved us
Sunrise is such a horrible thing
& yet

Every day
We are called & waiting
If fortune favors us, we may find ourselves.
Squeeze the life out of our hand
There is so much to be said
We don't believe we should
Ever get through
One year normal

Maybe we remember now.

All the schools, churches, theaters, dancing halls, etc.

Are closed here also.

There is a bill in the Senate.

We can't help but hope.

Ha! Ha!

If we are not dead

Write

Write

To be

To do

To—[†]

[†] To her friend at the Haskell Indian Nations University, Kansas,
October 17, 1918. Bureau of Indian Affairs.

[OURS]

To hand right respect
To the negroes—
To Father death.
Do not come for them.
This is our opinion—
As they are given
By the will, the word.
All negroes considered Debts,
Parts which we are entitled to.
A sort of epidemical cold
Has seized every business &
Establishment our health afflicted,
We have recovered,
The incision made
By this impost-
Hume has been cured.
Join us in every good.[‡]

---

‡ Letter from George Washington to Betty Washington Lewis,
October 12, 1789. National Archives.

SELMA EPP

They stood away.
Made their own sick.
People hoping—
God, take away the illness.
Everyone grew

Weaker & weaker.
The strongest carried
Everyone.
Protest.
Daniel was two;
He was just a little boy.
His body took him away.[§]

---

§ An account by Selma Epp, who was a child in a Jewish neighborhood
in North Philadelphia during the 1918 influenza epidemic.

THE DONOHUE FAMILY

Usually people
        Fall
People   dy
People   should not have died.
Most of them immigrants.
These people came Promised Land.
They came fresh

&   they got

Destroyed.¶

¶ Account of Michael Donohue, whose family ran a funeral home
when the 1918 influenza epidemic struck.

DONOHUE
FAMILY LEDGERS

Our common era can tell
Who a person was,
Where he lived, what he died of.
But we become sloppy
& confused, crossed out,
Scribbled in borders –
It's nearly impossible to track
Tragedy & turmoil.
We didn't.
We buried people we knew.
We buried strangers.
A girl.
To take care of people
Was the decent thing to do.
We had a responsibility.
Scribbled at the bottom
The 'girl,'
'This girl was buried in the trench.'
This girl was our trench.
Where else to put her.**

** Donohue on his Family Ledgers.

DC PUTSCH

The
Cap
itol
co
uld
feel the
tenseness it show
ed in the air glaring of t
he awful night before the
worst was yet to come—Wash
ington showed the plain dread
of going into something, we knew
not what. We moved about quietly—
grimly & entirely. We had experienced
varied emotions on making the nation,
but none like this. It was almost an imp
ossibility for us to realize as a truth that men
& women mobbed, chased, dragged, beat & killed within the

shadow of the dome of the Capitol, at the very front door of the White House. We had expected to find the people panicky; we found us terrified & afraid. Although some shots had blazed the night, we had reached the determination that we would defend & protect home & that determination rendered us calm. Still there was a tautness wild circulating terrible things—whatever they might be, the people had made up our minds to meet. Darkness had something to do with the things that did happen. The cause of the riots—It was plain that was the plan—call the seeds of a race riot by their action taken upon victims. The Capitol went over—not only local, but national causes of the trouble. Mob violence secure from these years—the promise that would father the same. Washington for perhaps the whole time stood as one struck dumb; a word scared through & through. The whites again took the aggressive. Surprise. Night returned disquieted, but not depressed; worse might have been a riot protected by the law. Run but fight—in defense of our lives. Feel the mark turning the whole nation.[††]

[††] From the article "The Riots: An N.A.A.C.P. Investigation," written by James Weldon Johnson in the NAACP's *The Crisis* magazine in 1919.

The Soldiers (or Plummer)
- .... . / ... --- .-.. -.. .. . .-. ...

How true to life,

All too true . . . you sing the Achaeans' fate,

All they did and suffered, all they soldiered through,

As if you were there yourself or heard from one who was.

—Robert Fagles (translator), *The Odyssey* (8.548–551)

Roy Underwood Plummer (1896–1966) was born in Washington, DC, & enlisted in the army in 1917. Corporal Plummer served in France in Company C of the 506th Engineer Battalion, which built roads, fortifications & conducted other manual labor that was essential to the army. Around 160,000 African American soldiers served as Services of Supply troops in France, enabling the critical supply & movement of white combat troops.

Plummer dutifully kept a diary throughout the war. His background as a clerk is exemplified by his precise understanding of grammar (he often crosses out or corrects himself, as if aware that someone else will be reading his work), impeccable handwriting & clear-cut descriptions of his experiences. Plummer's journal, housed at the National Museum of African American History and Culture, has been fully transcribed & digitized by the Smithsonian Transcription Center.

After the war, Plummer returned to Washington, DC, & practiced medicine in the District of Columbia for over forty years. ††

---

†† See caption on pages 116–117.

———————————————————————————Date 1/26/18

Called for first time for guard duty.

Bright moonlight

———————————————————————————

Call this a poem.

Teach us how to walk from war

Like we ever could.

———————————————————————————

———————————————————————————

———————————————————————————Date 6/2/18

There was this provision: "The walking of

white soldiers with colored women or

colored soldiers with white women within

the limits of this camp is strictly

prohibited."

Whites don't love mixing,

Race that launched a thousand whips.

Watch us bleed the night.

Epidemic of Spanish Influenza has been
raging. We now have 4 men in hospital
with it and 7 men are said to have died
in one night of it.

We hear men coughing

Then the stiff, loaded silence

Of coughing no more.

God, the symmetry.

Coughin' into their coffins.

Life takes breath away.

The dawn brushed back a curtain that
concealed in its folds a place that really
seemed deserving of the ~~name~~ term "God-
forsaken."

In this one-chance life,

Nothing is ever promised,

Not even the land.

We might stay a while

Cuz they don' kill us here bad

As they do back home.

12/1918

Friction between the races. Though the
colored troops are not equipped with
guns, according to all reports, they
behaved themselves most bravely and
pluckily against the Marines. It seems
that the trouble started in a cafe when a
Marine Sgt made some remark which
displeased the colored "boys" there and
resulted in the Sergeant's receiving a
severe trouncing.

The Sgt then really informed his men and
incited a riot. The Marines, it seems,
began to promiscuously beat up every
                    that
soldier of color who happened to be
alone and the colored boys reciprocated.
One colored soldier of Co. "A" 506,
stabbed by a bayonet in the affray, died
at the Camp Hospital about half an hour
later. It was reported that 2 or 3 white
soldiers were killed, and it is known
that there are 3 or 4 white fellows in
the hospital with "bad heads," as Wilbur
Halliburton put it. The fracas caused
quite a stir.

Account of Battles Engaged in

We are a riot,

Our black leaves some things ink-bright.

Watch us bleed just right.

So, if we must die,

Let it be as nothing less

Than what we ~~are~~ were.

....Date 1/4/19

Colder and extremely windy. Post up

delinquency records in forenoon. Very busy

these days, in fact, for last 5 or 6 mos.

Many rumors about returning home ever

since armistice was signed.

Our lives end from flu—

One must ask: Have we really

Won this war at all.   Date

Account of Battles Engaged in

1/5/19

There comes to mind in the way of a
severe reprimand, this little verse:

"Count that day lost
Whose low descending sun
Views from thy hands
No worthy action done."

However, this day was not lost, in any
sense of the word.

Action is joining
The weaponry of our hands.
Ready, aim higher.

Date 1/20/19

Much colder. Epidemic, said to be the

"Flu" raising sand with Co. "A". Quite

a number are sent to the Hospital.

Gulps of our lives,

Gargling from our treasured chests,

Going, going, gone.

Date

Dying is blinding;

It rips from our eyes, leaves them

Stars that won't stare back.

111

Quite a cold day; in fact, one of the

coldest that I have witnessed in France

Co "A" affected more by the Epidemic, is

placed under quarantine and a marine

guard posted around barracks.

Atlas, too, carried.

At last, something to die for.

Alas, we die fast.

Go to Headquarters (Bn) to work

forenoons owing to Headquarters force

being under quarantine.

They will keep sleeping,

Hard heads laid for good.

Death is no brief dream.

Autographs of Comrades

1/23/19

More than 60 men of Company "A" are in
the Camp Hospital with the new malady.
Cold. Co. "D" also placed under
quarantine.

All we've wanted, fled.

Alive: all we want to be,

All we cannot stay.

1/24/19

Still cold, and the epidemic still
spreading, especially in Company "A".
Our company dons "Flu" masks as a
preventive measure.

This brown-boned garden.

Limp stalks graved in rows.

Man, we feed this earth.

Addresses of Home Friends

1/26/19
. . . .

To date there are 116 men of Co. "A"
. . . .

in Hosp., 2 of whom, it is reported,
. . . .

died early this morning. A little snow
. . . .

today, not much.
. . . .

~~GO~~. America,
. . . .

Call us "All We Have Died For."
. . . .

Lord knows it's enough.
. . . .

. . . .

1/27/19
. . . .

Somewhat warmer. Our company is placed
. . . .

under quarantine and not allowed out
. . . .

of quarters except for duty. 3 or 4
. . . .

men are found with high fevers.
. . . .

Remembering what
. . . .

We've lived is its own tall fight.
. . . .

Memory's a mess.
. . . .

Headquarters force having returned, I

am relieved from duty at Bn. Hq.

When it's listened to,

Memory's a message in

Our bottled-bodies.

Oops, got the year wrong

This year is all wrong, all long.

Time takes us on.   Date

"Flu" masks are eliminated,

quarantine measures affecting this

company not very strict.

Armistice has come,

The battle not done:

Race riots will smoke our streets,

Our award for prevailing.

Fine is just not free.

We return fighting ....Date........

If return we do.

This flag calls us last.

The prose portions are his original diary entries, while the verses are my own creation, where I imagine new writings. In writing in Corporal Plummer's voice, I wanted to do so in a form that embodied his concise language. The lined papers used as a journal background in this piece

```
                                              6/5/19
·····································Date·······························

Honorably discharged. / Buy ticket

for Washington, D.C., arriving /

there early the / morning of the 6th.




                                              6/6/19
·····································Date·······························

Some have decided to leave,

We have decided to live,

Breathing a warred skin.

Life leaves us gasping.

Ships carry us to U.S.

Our wrists still shackled.

We drop our guns, not our grief.

We make home worth fighting for.
```

are scans of blank pages in Plummer's original diaries. The haiku was particularly fitting—many of Plummer's entries are one to three sentences, & the haiku is three lines, their five-seven-five syllable pattern demanding an economic use of language.

WAR: WHAT, IS IT GOOD?

.-- .- .-. / .-- .... .- - / .. ... / .. - / --. --- --- -..

How much toilet paper,
Hand sanitizer,
Were we allowed?
In battle, everything,
Even hope, is rare & rationed,
Creating competitors from comrades,
Making monsters of men.
This mask is our medal of honor.
It has our war written all over it.

* * *

The 1918 influenza killed 50 million people (though some scholars suggest it could be 100 million), far more than those killed in World War I. The death toll of the influenza was intrinsically tied to warfare. The movement of large numbers of troops across the continents contributed to the spread of the virus; meanwhile millions of noncombatants were uprooted from their homes. The influenza was particularly devastating to Indigenous communities, which had already barely survived ethnic

cleansing campaigns. No matter what we're told, violence
is never little.

* * *

War, like a whale, is all consuming—
Everything fits into its mesh mouth.
Like a whale, a virus can wolf
Down the globe whole.
The bullet is a beast, as are we.
Our invisible battles
Are the hardest ones to win.

* * *

The first step in warfare & pandemics is the same:
Isolation, to rupture the channels of communication of
virus/violence.

The British pioneered cable cutting during WWI, using
the CS *Alert* to dredge Germany's underwater telegraph
cables. Wartime censorship also slashed communication
& truth-telling; the US Sedition Act of 1918 outlawed
speech or expression that damaged the country's image or
war effort. Fearing punishment, newspapers minimized
the threat of the virus, often refusing to print doctors'
letters warning the public not to gather or travel. This

censorship & misinformation only contributed to the further communication of influenza across the country & globe. Fire barrel of the throat. Words, too, are a type of combat, for we always become what we refuse to say.

* * *

After we fight
Someone we love,
We offer a question:
Are we okay?
Are we good?
The First World War was once called "Great,"
So named "The War to End All Wars."
Ha.
What is called "great"
Is often grievous & gruesome,
But what is good is worth our words.
Good trouble.
Good fight.
Good will.
Good people.
To be good is to be larger than war.
It is to be more than great.

* * *

The body is a walking
Chaos of meat & bones.
Deaths & injuries in armed conflicts
Are called casualties, *casual* meaning
"By chance" or "accident."
But bloodshed in war is no misfire.
Perhaps *casualty* means that war itself
Is the accident, unmistakably a mistake,
Our big, fat, bloody *oops!*

* * *

The second step in warfare & pandemics
Is the same: continuation,
To uphold remaining modes of connection &
communication. Writing letters to the home front was
encouraged among WWI service personnel & volunteers
abroad so as to raise national morale. The British Army
Postal Service delivered around 2 billion letters during
their involvement in the conflict. In the US, 1917's
General Orders No. 48 stated that "Soldiers, sailors, and
marines assigned to duty in foreign countries are entitled
to mail letters 'free'"... by marking on the envelopes On

Active Service . . . During the war, A. E. F. Camp Crane in Allentown, Pennsylvania, reported its post office handling nearly 70,000 pieces of mail per week. The home front is a pen. Pen us in. We swear we can be good.

* * *

Listen closely.
Are you listening?
There is no such thing as gentle war.
There is no peace
That can't be flung aside.
Our only enemy is that which would
Make us enemies to each other.

* * *

Snail mail?
More like whale mail.
It is the only thing
With a mouth wide enough to speak
When we have nothing left
To say. All this to say,
Writing our stories
Is an essential service.
It is how we go to war.

Most importantly,
It is how we end it.
We're still willing to believe
Peace is a place on earth.

* * *

A century past World War I, condolence cards sold out
in 2020. A majority of United States Postal Service users
agree that receiving letters raises their spirits & one in six
send more mail now during the pandemic. In pandemics,
everything is scarce except for grief. Writing, truth-telling
to one another, is an act of hope-making when hope is
hardest found. What place have we in our histories except
the present.

* * *

Aperture:
The hole in the eye
Through which light travels.
The word *peace* shares history
With *pact*. That is to say, harmony
Is a tomorrow we agree on.

We're more conditioned

To contagion than combat.
But a virus, just like a war, separates us
From our fellow people.
　　　　Yet if we are willing, the cut
　　　　Can be an aperture, the hole
Through which we reach for the whole
Of one another.

A virus is fought inside us,
While violence is fought amongst us.
In both, our triumph is not in conquering others,
But conquering the most destructive agents
& instincts that we carry
Within our mortal forms.
Hate is a virus.
A virus demands a body.
What we mean is:
Hate only survives when hosted in humans.
If we are to give it anything,
Let it be our sorrow
& never our skin.
To love just may be
The fight of our lives.

The Ship

THE FELLOWSHIP

B Well

The ship calls you man. Bullet, refrain from going into public
places. Service is putting good to all civil rights, causes,
nations, our form. O order so vicious has been issued in many.
Democracy before war.

B Well[§§]

[§§] April 1918 letter from Mrs. Ida B. Wells-Barnett, President of the Negro Fellowship League,
to United States President Woodrow Wilson. In the letter she protests General Ballou's
Bulletin Number 35 for the 92nd Division, Camp Funston, Kansas, which urged officers &
soldiers of color against entering public places where they were unwanted due to their race.
National Archives.

_ _ _ _ R I P _ _ _ _ _ _
A _ _ _ _ _ SHIP

Fig. I.

a ship owed the last year

The numb act carried

on this ship follows the ship & the practice of man the utmost that can be stowed

in a vessel of men is men only insurrections are more than rest. The men carried

351 the number of men stated in the plan 190. Difference of 161. Women

boys girls here did carry each other. Dead morning. Height between

decks & platform 2 feet 7 inch a place has to lie & breathe in.

Numb fellow creatures used in their country to anguish

Fig. III

Fall sick die. The privilege
of being the little hope of
recovery. The ship bruised &
bows the women children the men
constantly chained two & two; each pair
ascend, solute this state, them being of change
being made to jump in their chains & this, by
friends, is called dancing. Carrying this human
flesh will appear rather a fiction than a real
representation of a ship. A humane man
would will the scar to be described.

Fig. VII

aint suffering those beings whom we want.
Country & captivity rendered blood & lux,
a slaughter-house. It is in the power of the
human imagination to picture itself carried,
restored. It had proved fatal to creep under
this infectious exhale from below a given sea.

Fig. V

A greater proportion of men perish in ONE year, than all the other years.

The time goes
passage from
person people
rip kept carried that
time. Humanity
must be univer
sal & lament
ed, a moral

and religious duty which may, without exaggeration, be the greatest on earth. *

It is said well that a sea is a grave for men *

* *Description of a Slave Ship*. London: Printed by James Phillips [for the London Committee of the Society for Effecting the Abolition of the Slave Trade], 1789. Two broadsides. This is perhaps the best-known depiction of a slave ship. Its images of enslaved Africans packed like sardines is most recognizable, while the narrative description printed below it, which is just as harrowing, rarely receives the same attention.

TEXT TILES: THE NAMES

Learn those lives touched
No one would touch you anymore, you said
Your friends had become afraid & could not hold you close.
The word is not in my vocabulary
Afraid is absent from our vocabulary
Is fate because of fear
We'll never know.
You know, don't you,
Even those you never knew remember you.

We will do our best to see
That no one will have to live without love
Know what it is like to be shunned
By nurses & friends, hospital employees
Refusing to come into your room
& when they did, they were covered in plastic gloves
& smocks.

Please take the pieces
Please forgive us for getting carried away.
We did it for two reasons—
For all who've been lost
& all who've lost them.
Fathers, grandparents, sisters, brothers,
Sons, daughters, nieces, nephews, lovers & friends
So good.
We could change things
We could stop the epidemic
We could save you
In the end, of course, we could not
Speak those names found by humanity.

Now cannot put love into the past tense
Above all, love—love very much.
If love could cure!
Each day slowly could not breathe.
Life still lives.
Our memories are you.
Remember this loving
Was dying.
Distort body
Breathing difficult
Lonesomeness is a never-ending ache.

We were barred from seeing
To see to mourn
We tried to forget.
We just can't let go yet
Hang on
Remember clearly
The best way is with poems
Remember
We were beginning
Dancing true
New meaning
New hope
We have held this hope with the rest.

We stood & did not see death.
Do you see
From the world to whatever awaits.¶¶

¶¶ This documentary poem was made using the letters of contributors to the AIDS
Memorial Quilt, each hand-sewn panel of which pays tribute to those who died from the
disease. First displayed in 1987, the Quilt is now part of the National AIDS Memorial.
As of 2021, it spans 1.2 million square feet & includes more than 48,000 panels.
According to UNAIDS, 27.2 to 47.8 million people have died from AIDS-related
illnesses globally since the start of the AIDS pandemic.

The Surveyed

REPORT ON MIGRATION
OF ROES

Welcome, Migrants, to Panpax.

As you are aware, Panpax, our idyllic country, has finally reopened its
gates to outsiders. We're aware that your nation Pandem, on the other
hand, is a low wasteland of sickness & death, where its people are
dubbed "roes" (a Pandemian derivative of "woes"). We've heard that
in Pandem all forms of gathering are prohibited, its reclusive citizens
don't even go so far as to share the same sidewalk, let alone breathe the
same air. Social-political life is quite different in Panpax & we're aware
that for this reason many of you roes have newly disembarked here
seeking refuge & refuge, a road forward, you shall have. Panpax City
Commissioners have conducted a series of interviews to document
the unique transitional experience of Pandem refugees now living
in Panpax. Our hope is that these condensed answers will help you
acclimate to our abundant nation. For their privacy, the names of roe
interviewees have been replaced with their respective numbers.

Sincerely,

Panpax President Pact

SURVEY

Migrants have been in their homes & met. Efforts have been made to learn why they came to Panpax & with what success they were themselves new.

Some of the replies to questions asked are given:

Question: What are you doing now in Panpax?
Answers:
    1. Looking.

Question: What have you been feeling?
Answers:
    2. Tired.
    19. Tired.

Question: In Pandem, what did you want?
Answers:
    10. Change.
    20. To get away.

Question: No. In Pandem, what did you want most?
Answers:
    5. People.

Question: Do you feel greater freedom & independence now in Panpax? In what ways? What can you do now that you couldn't before?

Answers:

1. Yes.
2. Yes.
3. Going to places of amusement & living.
5. Yes. Go anywhere you want to go; don't have to look, get off the street.
6. Yes. Just to feel a feeling of good fellowship.
8. Yes. Can go anyplace I like. In Pandem I was gated & not treated.
9. Yes. Privilege to mingle with people; can go to the parks & places of being.
11. Yes. If you went to an ice cream parlor for anything you came outside to eat it. Got off sidewalk for people.
12. Yes. feel free; haven't any fear.
16. Yes. Feel more like a man. Same as slavery, in a way, at Pandem. I don't have to give up the sidewalk here for people as in Pandem.
17. No restrictions as to shows, schools, etc.
20. Was not counted in Pandem; people allowed no freedom at all in Pandem.

Question: What were your first impressions when Panpax opened & you arrived?

Answers:

1. The air of doing things.
3. Full of life, went to see the sights every night for a month.
4. I thought it was some great place but found out it wasn't. Living nothing but a hole. Sure wished I was back home.
5. When I got on the street & saw people by people all over I just held my breath, for I thought any minute they would start, then I saw nobody notice & I just thought this was a real place for people. No, indeed, I'll never work in anybody but my own.
6. Was completely lost, friend was to meet me but didn't & I was afraid   where to go   so much noise running I rest.
8. Always liked Panpax, even the name before I came.
13. Thought it a good place for people to live in.
15. Didn't like it; lonesome, until I went out. Then liked the places which have no restrictions.
16. Like it even better now.
17. Think I will like it later on.

Question: In what respects is life harder or easier in Pandem than in Panpax?

Answers:

4. Easier, it means more to you.
7. I make money, but spend it all to live.
8. Find it easier to live because I have to.

10. The strain is not so great.

11. Harder here than at Pandem.

13. More work, work is harder. The necessities of life.

14. Shorter hours.

15. Would rather be here than in Pandem. I have shorter hours here.

17. Easier to live in Panpax.

20. The entire family feels that life is much easier in Panpax than anywhere.

Question: What do you like about Panpax?
Answers:

1. Freedom … but it ain't always safe.

4. Freedom allowed in every way.

7. Work, can work any place.

8. The schools for the children.

9. The chance people have to live.

10. The friendliness of people, health better.

13. Right to live.

14. Ability to live in peace; not held down.

18. People live & go more places than home.

19. Industrial & educational facilities.

20. Haven't found anything yet to like more than before.

Question: What difficulties do you think a person from Pandem meets in coming to Panpax?
Answers:

3. Getting used to living; not letting life run away with you.

4. Closeness.

5. Crowded.

6. Growing accustomed to people.

7. Getting used to the ways of people.

9. Know of no difficulties a person from Pandem meets coming to Panpax.

10. Persons would likely meet.

12. Adjustment to working.

13. Climactic changes.

14. Change in climate, crowded, lack of space.

16. Knowing where they are going to stop.

18. If they know the danger in getting among people.

20. If persons know what they are, come with the intention.

Question: How is your free time different in Panpax than in Pandem?

Answers:

1. The buying of clothes here. You can try on things; you can do that in stores.

2. Can go into almost any place.

3. I live more, feel more.

4. Yes. Wife can try on a hat & if she doesn't want it she doesn't have to keep it; go anywhere I please.

5. Ain't afraid to get on cars & sit where I please.

6. There are so many places to go here, but down Pandem you work, work, work & you save & you haven't any place to spend it.

7. Don't go out very much but like to know I can where & when I want to.

9. At Pandem did not go what few places people were allowed to go. Here, roes can want.
11. Have more comforts in the home that could not have at home.
17. Yes, more places to go, parks & playgrounds for children.
19. No comment.

Question: Are you advising friends that it is better if they move to Panpax?
Answers:
1. Yes. People don't really believe the things we write, I didn't believe myself until I got here.
2. No. I am not going to encourage them to come, for they might not make it.
6. Yes. I have two sisters. I am trying to get them to come here. They can't understand why I stay, but they'll see if they come.
7. People don't realize how some parts were awful where we came from; folks here ain't afraid to breathe.
8. Want friend & husband to come; also family who want to see how she looks before they break. Youngest son begs mother never to think of going back.

Only a few migrants were found who came free. Few expressed a desire to return.

The responses utilized in the previous poem are taken from the 1922 report *The Negro in Chicago*. The document is a thorough sociological study conducted by the Chicago Commission on Race Relations to understand the causes & effects of the devastating Chicago race riots of 1919, one of many inflection points of violence during what was dubbed "Red Summer." Chicago's conflict left twenty-three African Americans & fifteen white people dead, over five hundred injured & at least a thousand homeless. As a part of their post-study, the Chicago Commission interviewed African Americans who'd left the Jim Crow South for Chicago. The previous poem, from "SURVEY" on, repurposes the report's text. It uses fragments of these migrants' answers, excerpting & erasing parts to create a newfound poem. From the report, the terms *North* or *Chicago* were replaced with *Panpax*. *Back home* or the *South* were switched for the word *Pandem*. *Roes* was put in place of *Negroes*. The interviewee numbers are in accord with the number given to that answer in the original document. Certain questions have also been partly preserved (for example, "Do you feel greater freedom & independence in Chicago? In what ways?" became "Do you feel greater freedom & independence now in Panpax? In what ways?").

Panpax is a meshing of *pan*, a prefix from Greek meaning *all*, & *pax*, the Latin word for *peace*.

This poem & its pain are both imagined & as real as we are. That is to say, through some fictions we find fact; in some fantasies we discover ourselves & then some. Even without living it, a memory can live on in us. The past is never gone, just not yet found.

Grief, like glass, can be both a mirror & a window, enabling us to look both in & out, then & now & how. In other words, we become a window pain. Only somewhere in loss do we find the grace to gaze up & out of ourselves.

_ _ _ _ _ [GATED]

Ha, we're so pained,
We probably thought
That poem was about us
& not another. Now we see
It was for both—for all of us
Who have been othered.
Where we are is no less
Than where we've come from.
To be haunted is to be hunted
By a history that is still hurting,
Needing healing as much as we do.

& just like that, through poetry,
We have recalled what was not ours,
Made the past the same as our pang.
This may be the only way we learn.

* * *

We've spent generations quarantined,
Exiled from the places of each other,
Life locked out from us.

Call us
Colum-abused,
Columbusted,
Colonized,
Categorized,
Cleansed,
Controlled,
Killed,
Conquered,
Captured to the coast,
Crowded,
Contained,
Concentrated,
Conditioned,
Camped.

Never forget that to be alone
Has always been a price for some
& a privilege for others.

We have yielded
Centuries of sidewalk,

Trained in this tradition
Before we even lived it—
What it is to bow our heads
& make room for someone else's pride.
That ceding of the walkway
Was the concession of the world
To another's age-old white rite of passage.

* * *

We always ask questions of those who came before.
To be surveyed, then, is to have survived.

Question: Why did the chicken cross the road?
Answer: Because there was a white person coming down it.

* * *

How we are moved says everything
About what we are to each other.
Last year we stepped onto an elevator.
We politely asked the white lady behind us
If she could please take the next lift
To continue social distancing.
Her face flared up like a cross in the night.
Are you kidding me? she yelled,

Like we'd just declared
Elevators for us only
Or *Yous must enter from the back*
Or *No yous or dogs allowed*
Or *We have the right to refuse*
Humanity to anyone.
Suddenly it struck us:

Why it's so perturbing for privileged groups to follow
restrictions of place & personhood.
Doing so means for once wearing the chains their power
has shackled on the rest of us.

It is to surrender the one difference that kept them
separate & thus superior.

Meanwhile, for generations we've stayed home, [segre]
gated, kept out of parks, kept out of playgrounds, kept
out of pools, kept out of public spaces, kept out of outside
spaces, kept out of outer space, kept out of movie theaters,
kept out of malls, kept out of restrooms, kept out of
restaurants, kept out of taxis, kept out of buses, kept out of

beaches, kept out of ballot boxes, kept out of office, kept
out of the army, kept out of hospitals, kept out of hotels,
kept out of clubs, kept out of jobs, kept out of schools, kept
out of sports, kept out of streets, kept out of water, kept
out of land, kept out of kept in kept from kept behind kept
below kept down kept without life.

Some were asked to walk a fraction / of our exclusion for a
year & it almost destroyed all they thought they were. Yet
here we are. Still walking, still kept.

To be kept to the edges of existence is the inheritance of
the marginalized.

Non-being, i.e., distance from society—social distance—
is the very heritage of the oppressed. Which means to
the oppressor, social distance is a humiliation. It is to be
something less than free, or worse, someone less-than-white.

For what does the Karen carry but her dwindling power,
dying & desperate? Dangerous & dangling like a gun
hung from a tongue?

Fundamentally, supremacism means doing anything to
keep one's sole conceit,
Even if it means losing one's soul.
It means not wearing the mask that would save you, for
that would mean taking off one's privilege.
It means, always, choosing poisonous
　　　　Pride over
　　　　Preservation,

　　　　　　　　Pride over
　　　　　　　　Nation,

　　　　　　　　　　　Pride over
　　　　　　　　　　　Anyone or anything.

This realization is not ours.
It is.
Art, if fact,
Is both a method & a finding,
An answer in the inquiry.
It is what is found
& the manner in which it is discovered.

Anyone who has lived
Is an historian & an artifact,
For they hold all their time within them.
Reconciliation is in this record we make.

If we remember anything,
Let it be to remember.
A road forward
We shall have
If we keep
Walking.***

*** To this day, drivers are seven times less likely to halt at the crosswalk for African American pedestrians than for whites. See Courtney Coughenour et al.

Walking as a pedestrian involves "collaborative processes by which users of public space come to trust each other." See Nicholas H. Wolfinger.

The yielding of walkways & thus power in public spaces is not a "Black" or "historical" issue, but the contemporaneous bedrock of status interaction in shared spaces. Research has found that African Americans as well as Latinx pedestrians tend to yield to whites. Women often yield their path to men & dark-skinned women yield to lighter-skinned women. See Natassia Mattoon et al.

DISPLACEMENT

A.
We've come so far,
We say,
But we have further to go.
In physics, we're taught that
Displacement & distance differ.
Displacement is merely the space between
Where an object starts & where it ends.

A ——————— B

But distance is the total length
Of the path an object takes:

A   B

How far Sisyphus pushes that rock
Up its murky mound,

As well as the route it rolls down again.

A poem & how it runs

Through the body before leaving

Us something slightly more than we were.

Simply put, the rise & fall matter,

Conjoined, not canceling,

Expansion, not erasure.

It is only then that we can understand

How our distance from our worst selves

Is centuries & yet

We have not been displaced.

Yes.

We have gone further than we've come.

* * *

A part of ourselves is still barbed

& barbaric, a wired complex of greed.

There is also the element that is

Guided by good,

The way our blood

Is bracketed by veins.

According to legend,

There are two wolves inside us:

One half that must be fought

& one that must be fed.

One that must fall
& one that must never fail.

B.
That wretched summer
We were distempered as dogs,
But to be disturbed is to be moved,
Pushed toward progress.
Our disgust is a measurement
Of distance, a distaste for what was.
It is to grasp that we must never go back.
History is fractured & fractal.
Even when we've succumbed,
We have not surrendered.
We might fall.
We might rise,
Distant but undisplaced,
Traveling further than we shift.

What matters most is that
We find each other
In the lit-up space   between.

FURY & FAITH

For my particular grief
Is of so flood-gate and o'er-bearing nature
That it engluts and swallows other sorrows
And it is still itself.
                    —William Shakespeare, *Othello*

AMERICA™

A house divided cannot stand. To be divided, then, is to be devastated.

The fact of the matter is that our country seldom counts all who

Matter. This is why red seeps from our flag. We will say again that

Language matters. From the beginning, the colonized are kennings:

African American, Asian American, Native American (apparently

There is no White American). American & adjective, American &

Qualifier. The term split up () and dismantled, stripped & stripped.

Erasure demands a lifetime of rehearsal. Do you really understand what it is to be this dispensable body.

We recognize the sobs now for the flags they were. The jerk of our heads, as if waking from a dream—or a

Nightmare. You decide. *This is not the nation we built, at most not the nation we've known. Know.* Oh, no.

This is the nation we've sewn. It is our right to weep for the wound we've always been. A silent

Shock out of the blue: A hand hung to another or a head pillowed by a shoulder is by far worth more

Than anything we've won or wanted. When told we can't make a difference, we'll still make a sound.

FURY & FAITH

You will be told this is not a problem,
Not *your* problem.
You will be told now is not the time
For change to begin,
Told that we cannot win.

But the point of protest isn't winning;
It's holding fast to the promise of freedom,
Even when fast victory is not promised.

Meaning, we cannot stand up to police
If we cannot cease policing our imagination,
Convincing our communities that this won't work,
When the work hasn't even begun,
That this can wait,
When we've already waited out a thousand suns.
By now, we understand
That white supremacy
& the despair it demands
Are as destructive as any disease.

So when you're told that your rage is reactionary,
Remind yourself that rage is our right.
It teaches us it is time to fight.
In the face of injustice,
Not only is anger natural, but necessary,
Because it helps carry us to our destination.

Our goal is never revenge, just restoration.
Not dominance, just dignity.
Not fear, just freedom.
Just justice.

Whether we prevail is not determined
By all the challenges that are present,
But by all the change that is possible.

& though we are unstoppable,
If we ever feel we might fail,
If we be fatigued & frail,
When our fire can no longer be fueled by fury,
We will always be fortified by this faith,
Found in the anthem, the vow:

Black lives matter,
No matter what.
Black lives are worth living,
Worth defending,
Worth every struggle.
We owe it to the fallen to fight,
But we owe it to ourselves to never stay kneeling
When the day calls us to stand.

Together, we envision a land that is liberated, not lawless.
We create a future that is free, not flawless.
Again & again, over & over,
We will stride up every mountainside,
Magnanimous & modest.
We will be protected & served
By a force that is honored & honest.
This is more than protest.
        It's a promise.

ROSES

Riots are red
Violence is blue
We're sick of dying
How 'bout you

THE TRUTH IN ONE NATION

That telltale luminescent green vest—
His bike, cruising leisurely a second before,
Skidded   to   a   ha   l   t

Like a DJ's hand on his turntable.
The hunter had made his mark.
Mark the world & make it his.
Though we had nothing to hide,
We performed our innocence for him,
Placed it on full display like a buffet platter.
Here. Feast your eyes on this.
Look.
Look.
No, really.
Though we strobed
That we came in peace,
He was already at war.
Because aren't we all,
                    Always?

We blinked, stunned,
A doe before the rifle.
Didn't he recognize
Who we were,
Who we was?
A girl just trying to walk home
& live to tell the tale.
In that moment, we desperately want
To snort

       To scream

          To survive.

We have battled hard to be.
Nothing—
& we mean nothing—
Can keep you safe.
Silence least of all.
Speak with this giant life,
For we might never be granted
That same breath again.

* * *
A nation's cold pride will kill,
Choke us on the very spot we shadow.
This is also called Chauvin[ism].

Such pain patrols with pattern,
Practiced, cooled, coded, familiar & un-familial.
Would we crave peace
If we knew what it was.
* * *
Our war has changed.
Whoever said we never die
In our dreams obviously
Has never been Black.
Sometimes the whole dusk pulls us down.

Sometimes in the thick
Of night we say our name
Again & again & again
Until it loses all its meaning,
Until its syllables are just
Another dead thing.
This is a rehearsal of sorts.

We stand still,
If just to insist
That we still
Exist.
Hoodied by a nightmare,
We resurrect ourselves.

* * *

Union of unwilling martyrs.
Death is no equalizer,
Death equals nothing,
Makes a 0 of a life.
That is the machinery of this country.

As the regular sprang back,
So did the violence,
Normal in its abnormality,
Completely unshuttered.
& so we were un-shuddering,
Our shoulders no longer recalling
How to ripple
After seeing our bodies

Ripped apart.
R. I. P.
Ravaged In Pandemic.
Rifled Innocent People.
Razed Irreplaceable Persons.
Look alive, everyone.
 * * *
To ask a question
Is to put our hand up
& ready ourselves for the end.
An answer is an assault,
It can knock you dead.
Can we tell you something? we ask.
Shoot! cracks the response.

O how our beloveds are besieged.
Despite how hard we've prayed,
Anyone becomes prey
            When they do not
Turn & run.
Nowadays, living
Is a dying art.

* * *

We were brought here
& all we got was this lousy T-shirt,
This drowsy, free hurt.
Taste our tired, unbroken rage.
Nothing we have witnessed
This lifetime surprises us.

Disbelief is a luxury
We never possessed,
A pause that never was.
How many times have we wheezed
A dread to last all night long.
The truth is, one nation under guns.

* * *

This republic was bred shady.
Country of guns & germs & steal-
ing land & life.
O say can we see
The blood we stand on,
Shining below us
Like a blood-slick star.
What we might've been if only we'd tried.

What we might become, if only we'd listen.
* * *
Scars & stripes.
Schools scared to death,
School drills of death.
The truth is, one education under desks,
Stooped low from bullets.
Soon comes the sharp plunge
When we must
Ask where our children
Shall live
& how.
         & if.

Who else shall we let perish.
* * *
Again, language matters.
Children have been taught—
America: without her, democracy fails.
But the truth is:
America without her democracy fails.

We thought our country would burn.
We thought our country would learn.

America,
How to sing
Our name,
Singular,
Signed,
Singed.

Ash is alkaline, meaning basic.
All too true.
Perhaps to burn is the most basic
Purification there is.
Time said: *You must transform to survive.*
We said: *Not over our dead body.*
What can we call a country that destroys
Itself just because it can?
A nation that would char
Rather than change?
Our only word for this is
Home.

* * *

There is more than one hue of haunting.
We want to believe that
What we care for can keep.

We want to believe.
The truth is, we are one nation, under ghosts.
The truth is, we are one nation, under fraud.
Tell us, honestly:
Will we ever be who we say.
* * *
The world still terrifies us.
We're told to write what we know.
We write what we're afraid of.
Only then is our fear
Made small by what we love.

Every second, what we feel
For our people & our planet
Almost brings us to our knees,
A compassion that nearly destroys
Us with its massiveness.
There is no love for or in this world
That doesn't feel both bright & unbearable,
Uncarriable.
* * *
We built this place,
Knowing it could lead,

Knowing it might not last,
Knowing it might lose.

Our people,
We take thee to have & to scold,
To love & to change,
In sickness & in health,
Till breath do us part.
How do we pronounce you,
Land & Strife?
Our hands must not lay
Down what they've begun.
* * *
Young, our country seems,
& stumbling, but striking,
Like a lion learning its legs.
One nation, blunder-pawed.

What we have not done delicately,
At least let us do decently & deliberately,
For there is still a promise here
We have promised here of all.
* * *

Some days we believe
In nothing
But belief. But
It is enough to carry us forward.

We believe we can transform
Without war or wariness.
We are stubborn, not simple.
Strategic, like a general who sees
They may not win this battle.
We're optimistic, not because we have hope,
But because only by being optimistic can hope
Be ours to have.
* * *
Grief depends on love.
What we cherish most shall leave.
But what we've changed can last,
Chartered & chosen.

We imagine us
& all we'll make of one another:
Our faces wet & shimmering
Like an open wound,

Dazed by the flare
Of our new-made selves.
The truth is: one world, wonder-awed,
Raw with revelation.
May such a prayer,
A people,
A peace,
A promise,
Be ours.
Be right
& radiant
& real.

LIBATIONS

After Layli Long Soldier

Today

as we

listen to   speak to

the past   the pain   the pandem

we call out   we carry on   we arc   we move

remembering   renaming   resisting   repairing   rousing

our world   our world   our world   our world

like haunts   like hulls   like humans

loosening   lighting

our mouths

home

RESOLUTION

In the beginning was the word.

—John 1:1

THE MIRACLE OF MORNING

We thought we'd awaken to a world in mourning.
Heavy clouds crowding, a society storming.
But there's something different on this golden morning.
Something magical in the sunlight, wide & warming.

We see a dad with a stroller taking a jog.
Across the street, a bright-eyed girl chases her dog.
A grandma on a porch fingers her rosaries.
She grins as her young neighbor brings her groceries.

While we might feel small, separate & all alone,
Our people have never been more closely tethered.
The question isn't *if* we can weather this unknown,
But *how* we will weather this unknown together.

So, on this meaningful morn, we mourn & we mend.
Like light, we can't be broken, even when we bend.

As one, we will defeat both despair & disease.
We stand with healthcare heroes & all employees;

With families, libraries, waiters, schools, artists;
Businesses, restaurants & hospitals hit hardest.

We ignite not in the light, but in lack thereof,
For it is in loss that we truly learn to love.
In this chaos, we will discover clarity.
In suffering, we must find solidarity.

For it's our grief that gives us our gratitude,
Shows us how to find hope, if we ever lose it.
So ensure that this ache wasn't endured in vain:
Do not ignore the pain. Give it purpose. Use it.

Read children's books, dance alone to DJ music.
Know that this distance will make our hearts grow fonder.
From these waves of woes our world will emerge stronger.

We'll observe how the burdens braved by humankind
Are also the moments that make us humans kind;
Let each morning find us courageous, brought closer;
Heeding the light before the fight is over.
When this ends, we'll smile sweetly, finally seeing
In testing times, we became the best of beings.

AUGURY
or THE BIRDS

In ancient Rome, augurs were official diviners,
Their darting eyes interpreting
Omens & the inked stain
Of birds across the sky.
Their job was not to prophesy the future,
But to determine if their new-named gods
Approved of an action before it began.

The only way to correctly predict
The future is to pave it,
        Is to brave it.
The breakage is where we begin.
The rupture is for remembering.
That is to say,
Here is where we hold our hurt.
We inaugurate our dreams at the injury.
We consecrate at the cut.
Under a suture of sun,

We sense ourselves stir,
Slowly, sweetly,
As if for the first time.
This nearly tore us apart.
Yes, indeed.
It tears us to start.

PRACTICE MAKES PEOPLE

The making of plans,
When this is over,
The *We can't wait,*
Really our knuckles rapping
Against the future, sounding
Out what lies beneath its hull.
But tomorrow isn't revealed,
Rather rendered, refined. Wrought.
Remember that fate isn't fought
Against. It is fought for. Again
& again.
* * *
Maybe there is no fresh wisdom,
Just old woes,
New words to name them by
& the will to act.
We've seen life lurching back in stops & starts
Like a wet-born thing learning to walk.
The air charged & changed.
Us, charged & changed.

A yoked-out eternity
For that needle to pierce our arm.
At last: a pain we asked for.
Yes, it is enough to be moved
By what we might be.

ANONYMOUS

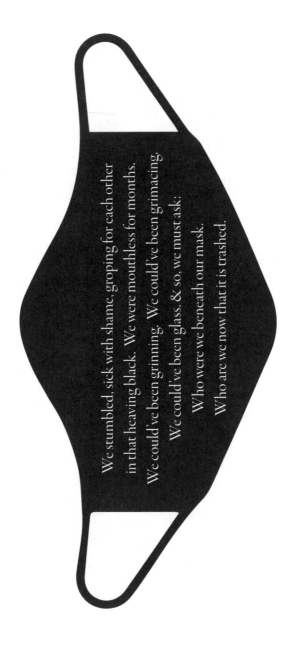

We stumbled, sick with shame, groping for each other
in that heaving black. We were mouthless for months.
We could've been grinning. We could've been grimacing.
We could've been glass, & so, we must ask:
Who were we beneath our mask.
Who are we now that it is trashed.

WE WRITE

Our hands splay toward some
Hazy & far-flung happiness
& we cleave open for some fragile
Non-evil, no matter how brief:
To touch,
To meet,
To human
Again; a scatter of non-particular
Wonders to be revisited.
All these unutterable blessings we forfeited—
Hugs, hope, heart—
Finally beloved by all & belittled by none.
It will take a whole fleet
Of words to return.

* * *

Then comes the thrust of our throats:
There is no more revenge
We shall boast, no matter
How heavily bladed in our fingers.

Change is made of choices,
& choices are made of character.
Cling to whatever brings us to begin,
Even if it is formless as foam.
We keep hoping
For no reason at all.
For every reason we share.

It is loss, as well as logic,
When we cry:
May those laid to rest never leave us,
            But lead us to rise.
We lived.
& that was more than we asked for.
We, too, must howl ourselves ablaze.

* * *

We write
Because you might listen.
We write because
We are lost
& lonely,
& you, like us,
Are looking
& learning.

MONOMYTH

A film is not what happened, a film is an impression
of what happened.   —Dustin Lance Black

SCENE 1: THE KNOWN WORLD

The part of the narrative where we see our hero as they see the
world. We understand "normal" in terms of how we believe a story
begins.

Dec. 2019: A new pneumonia-like illness is identified in Wuhan,
China (& though we aren't aware of it yet, a patient treated in France
in late December too has the coronavirus).

Dec. 18: Australia experiences its hottest day on record, following
its driest spring.

SCENE 2: THE CALL

Our hero is summoned to some call that bends beyond the horizon.
Will they follow, the audience ponders, munching on their popcorn.
Only you can answer that.

Jan. 2020: Australia's apocalyptic brushfire season garners
international attention. Over the course of the crisis, an estimated
46 million acres are burnt, thirty-three lives lost & 3,094 homes

destroyed. The World Wildlife Fund estimates in January that over a billion animals die. Burning of the Amazon rain forest & deforestation across the globe continue. In 2020, around 10,900 square kilometers of forest—more than 2 million US football fields—will be cut down.

Jan. 30: The World Health Organization (WHO) declares a global health emergency.

SCENE 3: REFUSAL OF THE CALL
The hero rejects the summoning. They are indolent, intimidated, or both. They are not yet what the story demands they become.

Feb. 7: Dr. Li Wenliang, a Chinese doctor who tried to warn the public early on about COVID-19, dies after contracting the virus. In early January, the authorities had forced him to sign a statement denouncing his concerns as unfounded. Use flashbacks as both foreshadowing & dramatic irony.

SCENE 4: THE MENTOR
A teacher appears, bone-deep with knowledge. They would have our hero learn what they have never known, never questioned.

Dr. Anthony Stephen Fauci speaks center stage.

SCENE 5: CROSSING THE THRESHOLD
Our hero enters the new realm, the winding wood, the perilous path. There is no turning back, or else we turn our back on ourselves.

The Ides of March: The *Grand Princess* cruise ship is held at sea. In Italy, people sing off their balconies. Here, the music swells in the soundtrack, soft & undying. On March 11, the WHO declares COVID-19 a pandemic. On March 13, Breonna Taylor, a twenty-six-year-old emergency medical technician in Louisville, Kentucky, is killed by police officers during a botched raid on her home. She is not the target of the raid, nor was the target there. A total of thirty-two rounds are fired by the officers' service weapons. It takes time for us to learn Taylor's name & even longer to say it.

Borders seal, social distancing, lockdown & quarantine are the lay of the land. By March 26, the US has more reported infections than any other country, disproportionately killing people of color, the working class & the incarcerated. By April 2, there have been more than 1 million confirmed cases in 171 countries. Nearly 10 million Americans lose their jobs. Show close-ups of people scavenging for toilet paper, children at home chewing on absolutely nothing.

SCENE 6: THE ROAD OF TRIALS
Obstacles bloom at every step, curved outward like weeds. We must adapt or fail.

In May, Japan & Germany both enter recessions. Cases rise in Latin America, deaths in the US pass 100,000, still the most of any nation. We are desperate to flatten the curve. Oh, how we miss curving into each other.

SCENE 7: THE DEDICATION
Loss strikes, loud & irrevocable as a gunshot. We must dedicate ourselves to our dead, march onward since they cannot.

May 25: George Floyd, a forty-six-year-old African American man, is killed in police custody as an officer kneels on his neck, ignoring his pleas that he can't breathe.

May 26: Black Lives Matter protests begin in Minneapolis & spread around the world. All over, we scream. We keep screaming.

SCENE 8: THE PINCH

A surprise, like suddenly looking down & seeing a knife sprout from your gut. This, among storytellers, is called a twist.

June 11: Coronavirus cases in Africa top 200,000.

July 10: We are numb & numbered. The US reaches 68,000 new cases in a day, shattering its single-day record for the seventh time in eleven days. Cut to a wide shot of a flag wearing a rusted gold medal.

July 13: By now, more than 5 million Americans have lost their health insurance.

SCENE 9: THE DARKEST MOMENT

There is no question about it: We have failed one another in the worst way. All seems lost. We are trapped in the trench; even crawling is beyond us.

Aug. 22: Global virus deaths surpass 800,000. Body after body after body after

Sep. 2020: Wildfires across California, Oregon & Washington make up the worst fire season on record, leading the states to experience some of the worst air quality on the planet (in some areas of Oregon, the air hazards actually surpassed the Air Quality Index). The fires burn more than 10.2 million acres of land, destroy over 10,000 buildings & kill almost forty people.

Sep. 3: The virus surges at US colleges, totaling more than 51,000 cases.

Sep. 7: India, with more than 4 million infections, becomes the nation with the second-highest number of cases.

Sep. 28: Global deaths reach 1 million, no doubt an underestimation.

Oct. 11: The world records more than 1 million new cases in three days.

SCENE 10: POWER WITHIN
The hero clenches their fist. Something tightens inside us like a muscle, a trembling memory reminds us of who & what we are. The music crescendos out of our bones. None of this is normal. Then again, neither are we.

Nov. 7: Joe Biden wins the US presidential election.

Dec. 2: The UK issues emergency-use authorization for Pfizer's coronavirus vaccine, becoming the first Western country to do so, & begins vaccinations on Dec. 8.

Dec. 6: COVID-19 outranks heart disease as the leading cause of death in the US.

Dec. 11: The FDA grants an emergency authorization for vaccines by Pfizer & will later do the same for Moderna on the 18th.

Dec. 14: The US death toll surpasses 300,000. Sandra Lindsay, a New York–based intensive care nurse, becomes the first person to receive a COVID vaccine in the US outside a clinical trial. She describes how important it was for her to get the shot as a Black woman. One governor says that this is the weapon that will end the war. As we soon see, the war has just begun.

SCENE 11: BATTLE
Our hero must engage in a battle between opposing forces. Armed with sword, saber, wands & words, they must defend what they believe in.

Jan. 6: Trump supporters storm the US Capitol, leading to the deaths of five people. Somewhere a poet writes in moonless light & all at once puts her pen down.

Jan. 7–8: Facebook & Instagram suspend Trump (later in June it is announced that this ban is for two years, ending in 2023). Twitter permanently bans Donald Trump for violating its glorification of violence policy.

SCENE 12: CLIMAX

Everything, it seems, has built up to this—a climax, a climb, high enough for us to see the pain, as well as the plain past it.

Jan. 20: Ext. Capitol Building—Day. Joe Biden is inaugurated as the forty-sixth president of the US, with Kamala Harris becoming the first-ever female vice president, as well as the first Asian American & African American to hold said position. Amanda Gorman, a skinny Black girl descended from slaves, becomes the youngest inaugural poet in US history. At exactly noon, sheer gray clouds bend & break for the day.

SCENE 13: RESOLUTION

The hero wipes down their sword, counts the dead. They are heading home, back to where it began. Head held high & bowed at the same time, they will never forget what happened here.

Jan. 20 continued: Construction of the Keystone XL pipeline is halted after President Biden revokes the permit of the project, which had planned to carry 800,000 barrels of oil from Alberta to the Texas Gulf Coast. Hours after his inauguration, President Biden announces in a letter to UN Secretary-General Antonio Guterres that the US will remain a member of the WHO, canceling the withdrawal planned by the previous administration.

Feb. 19: The US rejoins the Paris Climate Agreement.

Feb. 27: The FDA issues an emergency use authorization for the Johnson & Johnson (J&J) COVID vaccine.

March 11: A year after the WHO declared COVID-19 a pandemic.

March 12: The United States administers its 100 millionth vaccine. Cases drop.

April 13: President Biden announces that he will withdraw all US forces from Afghanistan by Sep. 11, the twentieth anniversary of 9/11, ending the country's longest war. In August, the Taliban will take control of Kabul.

April 20: George Floyd's killer is convicted on two counts of murder & one count of manslaughter. All over, we weep.

By late July, almost 4 billion vaccination doses have been administered worldwide. We unglue our foreheads from our knees, tug our hands away from our faces like masks. Beneath them our smiles are stripped down like breastplates after war.

Somewhere a reader reads this.
Does resolution exist if it is ongoing, unwritten, unread?
The part of the narrative where we see our hero as they see the world.
We understand "normal" in terms of how we believe a story begins.
Inspirational, insightful, inside us.
There is always someone missing from the music.

SCENE 14: THE UNORDINARY WORLD

The hero is different. Their universe is different. There is something new perched on the edge of the earth like a sun.

Hint at the movie's sequel, *DELTA VARIANT,* coming later this year, as well as the third installment, *LAMBDA.*
Blackout.
Narrator's voice rambles, soaking up the silence.
Cue protagonist theme melody from the beginning for a good bookend.
At the end of their journey, a hero may stand in the same place where their story started, but nevertheless they have been irrevocably shifted, altered, displaced.

We are not all heroes, but we are all at least human. This is not a closing, but an opening, a widening—not a yawn but a scream, a poem sung. What will we admit of & into ourselves. There is no such thing as "all over" or "all done." If we are brought any closure, it will be in us being brought closer. Oh, how neat & needed strife seems when it is storied. How we send a clean-carved arc on & on. Our tales are how this world is passed.

This timeline, naturally, will never be complete. The sample is never simple, is always insufficient at invoking the insufferable.
There is no one way to count who & what counted most to us in that dark.

These are but some of the things we overcome.
But let us come to be more than their sum.

CODA IN CODE

_ O _ _ PEN!

NOW _ PEN!

_ _ _ _ _ IT IS OVER

_ _ _ WA_T IS OVER

THANKS FOR _ ASKING!

FIN _ _ _ _

_ _ LAST

_ _ _ ALLY

_ _ COME BACK

WE _ COME BACK

WE_ _ _ _ _ _ _ _ _ _ _ _ _ _ _ WILD

WE_ _ _ _ RING

WAT_ _ _ _ _ _ _ _ _ _ _ _ _ _ _ WE_ _
MEANT TO _ SEE_

WAT_ _ _ _ _ _ _ _ _ _ _ _ _ _ _ WE_
MEANT TO BE _ _ _ _ ^†††

††† Key: The letters in this puzzle are taken from business advertisements we saw June through July 2021. People with auditory processing disorders, like the author, often have difficulty processing & recalling the order of sounds & words. The original ads for the third to last & last two sentences were, respectively:

Welcome back to the wild (advertisement for a zoo)

Watch movies like they were meant to be seen (advertisement for a movie theater)

THE UNORDINARY WORLD

The worst is over,
Depending on who you ask.
This time, we are alone,
Not by command,
But because all we've ever desired
Is a second of our own,
To be still & seeing,
Remote but non-distant,
Like a moon orbiting
The globe it's most fond of.

Now that the best has begun,
Depending on who you ask,
We will be no worm,
Shrinking from all that shines.
Our future is a sea
Flooded with sun,
Our souls, so solar & soldiering.
There is a cut of that burning in us all.
Who are we, if not
What we make of the dark.

ESSEX II

As the world came apart,
      We have come together.
Only we can save us.
      Our faces fill with the hour,
New meaning lapping
      Against us like mooned tides.
Laden with what we've lost,
      We are led
By what we love.
      As far away as it is,
The late sun looks
      Peelable in our palm.
That is to say, distance
      Renders all massiveness
Carriable. It is the carrying
      That makes memory mutual,
The pain both private & public.
      Slowly, grief becomes a gift.
When we greet it, when we listen to our loss,
      When we indeed let it live,

It will not shrink in size,
       But lighten in load.
It lets us breathe.
       The densest despair takes
Us to no ordinary joy.
       Sometimes diving
Into the deep inside us
       Is the only way
We rise above it.

RESOLUTE

This rush of peace runs
So deep it roots us to the spot.
It is true that poetry
Can lamp an era scraped hollow,
A year we barely swallowed.
There is a justice in joy,
Starlit against all that
We have ended, endured &
Entered.
We will not stir stones.
We shall make mountains.

ARBORESCENT III, or ELPIS

Let us rephrase,
For we'll say it right this time
(& isn't that what endings are for?):
We do not hope for no reason.
Hope is the reason for itself.
We don't care for our beloveds
For any specific, singular logic,
But, rather, for the whole of them.
That is to say,
Love is justified by loving.
Like you, we are haunted & human.
You, like us, are haunted & healing.
What we feel to be true
Can only be understood
By what it does to the body.
The same as trees,
We, too, are shaped
By how we twist
Toward all that shoots
Us through with sun.

We truly are growing
Up & out of this hurt
If we'd rather char
Than chain this love.
Our only word for this is
Change.

CLOSURE

To begin again
Isn't to go backwards,
But to decide to go.
Our story is not a circle carved,
But a spiral shed/shaped/spinning,
Shifting inward & outward *ad infinitum*,
Like a lung on the bank of speech.
Breathe with us.
We disembark both beside & beyond
Who we were, who we are.
It is a return & a departure.
We spiral on, pushing up & out,
Like a growing thing
Making its form out of earth.
In a poem, there's no end,
Just a place where the page
Glows wide & waiting,
Like a lifted hand,
Poised & paused.

Here is our bond, unbordered by bone.
Perhaps love is how it feels
To breathe the same air.
All we have is time, is now.
Time takes us on.
How we are moved says everything
About what we are to each other
& what are we to each other
If not everything.

WHAT WE CARRY

As kids we sat in grass,
Fished our hands into the dirt.
We felt that damp brown
Universe writhe, alert & alive,
Earth cupped in the boat of our palms.

Our eyes waxed wide with wonder.
Children understand:
Even grime is a gift,
Even what is mired is miraculous,
What is marred is still marvelous.

Ark: a boat like that which preserved Noah's family &
animals from the flood. The word comes from the Latin
word *arca*, meaning "chest," much like the Latin word
arcere, "to close up, defend, or contain." *Ark* can also mean
the traditional place in a synagogue for the scrolls of the
Torah.

That is to say,
We put words in the ark.
Where else to put them.
We continue speaking/writing/hoping/living/loving/
fighting.
That is to say, we believe beyond disaster.

Even endings end
At the lip of land.
Time arcs into itself.
It is not a repeat, but a reckoning.
Days can't help but walk two by two—
The past & present, paired & paralleled.
It is the future we save
From ourselves, for ourselves.

Words matter, for
Language is an ark.
Yes,
Language is an art,
An articulate artifact.
Language is a life craft.
Yes,

Language is a life raft.

We have recalled how to touch each other
& how to trust all that is good & all right.
We have learned our true names—
Not what we are called,
But what we are called
To carry forth from here.
What do we carry, if not
What & who we care most for.

What are we,
If not the price of light.
Loss is the cost of loving,
A debt more than worth every pulse & pull.
We know this because we have decided to
Remember.

The truth is,
One globe, wonder-flawed.
Here's to the preservation
Of a light so terrific.
The truth is, there is joy

In discarding almost everything—
Our rage, our wreckage,
Our hubris, our hate,
Our ghosts, our greed,
Our wrath, our wars,
On the beating shore.
We haven't any haven
For them here. Rejoice, for
What we have left
Behind will not free us,
But what we have left
Is all we need.
We are enough,
Armed only
With our hands,
Open but unemptied,
Just like a blooming thing.
We walk into tomorrow,
Carrying nothing
But the world.

THE HILL WE CLIMB

Mr. President and Dr. Biden, Madam Vice President and
Mr. Emhoff, Americans, and the World:

When day comes, we ask ourselves:
Where can we find light
In this never-ending shade?
The loss we carry, a sea we must wade.

We've braved the belly of the beast.
We've learned that quiet isn't always peace,
And the norms and notions of what "just is"
                              Isn't always justice.

And yet the dawn is ours before we knew it.
                    Somehow, we do it.
Somehow, we've weathered and witnessed
A nation that isn't broken, but simply unfinished.

We, the successors of a country and a time
Where a skinny Black girl,

Descended from slaves and raised by a single mother,
Can dream of becoming president,
Only to find herself reciting for one.

And yes, we are far from polished, far from pristine.
But this doesn't mean we're striving to form a union that is
    perfect.
We are striving to forge our union with purpose,

To compose a country committed
To all cultures, colors, characters,
And conditions of man.
And so we lift our gazes not
To what stands between us,
But what stands before us.
We close the divide,
Because we know to put
Our future first, we must first
Put our differences aside.

We lay down our arms
So that we can reach our arms out to one another.
We seek harm to none, and harmony for all.

Let the globe, if nothing else, say this is true:
That even as we grieved, we grew,
That even as we hurt, we hoped,
That even as we tired, we tried.
That we'll forever be tied together. Victorious,
Not because we will never again know defeat,
But because we will never again sow division.

Scripture tells us to envision that:
"Everyone shall sit under their own vine and fig tree,
And no one shall make them afraid."
If we're to live up to our own time, then victory
Won't lie in the blade, but in all the bridges we've made.
That is the promised glade,
The hill we climb, if only we dare it:
Because being American is more than a pride we inherit—
It's the past we step into and how we repair it.

We've seen a force that would shatter our nation rather
    than share it,
Would destroy our country if it meant delaying
    democracy.
And this effort very nearly succeeded.

But while democracy can be periodically delayed,
It can never be permanently defeated.

In this truth, in this faith, we trust.
For while we have our eyes on the future,
History has its eyes on us.

This is the era of just redemption.
We feared it at its inception.
We did not feel prepared to be the heirs
Of such a terrifying hour.
But within it we've found the power
To author a new chapter,
To offer hope and laughter to ourselves.

So while once we asked: How could we possibly prevail
   over catastrophe?
Now we assert: How could catastrophe possibly prevail
   over us?

We will not march back to what was,
But move to what shall be:
A country that is bruised but whole,

Benevolent but bold,
Fierce and free.

We will not be turned around,
Or interrupted by intimidation,
Because we know our inaction and inertia
Will be the inheritance of the next generation.
Our blunders become their burdens.
But one thing is certain:
If we merge mercy with might, and might with right,
Then love becomes our legacy,
And change, our children's birthright.

So let us leave behind a country better than the one we
    were left.
With every breath from our bronze-pounded chests,
We will raise this wounded world into a wondrous one.

We will rise from the gold-limned hills of the West!
We will rise from the windswept Northeast, where our
    forefathers first realized revolution!
We will rise from the lake-rimmed cities of the
    Midwestern states!
We will rise from the sunbaked South!

We will rebuild, reconcile, and recover,
In every known nook of our nation,
In every corner called our country,
Our people diverse and dutiful.
We'll emerge, battered but beautiful.

When day comes, we step out of the shade,
Aflame and unafraid.
The new dawn blooms as we free it,
For there is always light,
If only we're brave enough to see it,
If only we're brave enough to be it.

NOTES

FUGUE

The line "tryna end things" is inspired by a lyric from the song "Work" by
Rihanna featuring Drake, which was released on the 2016 album *Anti*.
Their lyrics are "If you come over / Sorry if I'm way less friendly."

"levels of social trust": David Brooks, "America Is Having a Moral
Convulsion," *The Atlantic*, October 5, 2020, https://www.theatlantic
.com/ideas/archive/2020/10/collapsing-levels-trust-are-devastating
-america/616581.

"a 2021 study suggests": Arnstein Aassve et al., "Epidemics and Trust: The
Case of the Spanish Flu," *Health Economics* 30, no. 4 (2021): 840–857,
https://doi.org/10.1002/hec.4218.

CUT

The lines "We must change / This ending in every way" were inspired by the
final sentence in Rainer Maria Rilke's poem "Archaic Torso of Apollo,"
which reads "You must change your life."

WHAT A PIECE OF WRECK IS MAN

"What a piece of wreck is man" is a phrase inspired by a monologue by
Prince Hamlet in William Shakespeare's play *Hamlet*, which reads
"What a piece of work is a man!"

ESSEX I

The line "we become what we hunt" is inspired by this passage from Nathaniel Philbrick's *In the Heart of the Sea: The Tragedy of the Whaleship Essex*: "The sperm whales' network of female-based family unit resembled, to a remarkable extent, the community the whalemen had left back home on Nantucket. In both societies the males were itinerants. In their dedication to killing sperm whales the Nantucketers had developed a system of social relationships that mimicked those of their prey."

ANOTHER NAUTICAL

"Wine-dark" is an epithet frequently used by Homer in *The Iliad* and *The Odyssey* to describe the sea.

LIGHTHOUSE

Terence was a formerly enslaved person who went on to become a famous playwright around 170 B.C.E. This line, "*Homo sum, humani nihil a me alienum puto*," is one of his most famous, and translates to "I am a man, I consider nothing that is human alien to me." Maya Angelou mentioned this quotation in Oprah's Masterclass series.
The line "No human is a stranger to us" calls back to Terence's sentiments.

HEPHAESTUS

The line "This is not an allegory" speaks to a quote from Plato's *Republic* (translated by Paul Shorey) on Hephaestus being cast from heaven by Zeus: "But Hera's fetterings by her son and the hurling out of heaven of Hephaistos by his father [Zeus] when he was trying to save his mother from a beating, and the battles of the gods in Homer's verse are things that we must not admit into our city either wrought in allegory or without allegory. For the young are not able to distinguish what is and what is not allegory."

CORDAGE, or ATONEMENT

For continuity of the book's voice, for many quotations and original
 documents used in the erasure poems, I have inputted the ampersand in
 place of "and," as well as the first-person plural "our/we/us" instead of
 other narrative pronouns. Punctuation and capitalization have also been
 modified occasionally where appropriate.
Hensleigh Wedgwood, *A Dictionary of English Etymology*, vol. 1 (London:
 Trübner & Co., 1859), 72.

EARTH EYES

The line "how we want our parents red" is inspired by Federico Garcia
 Lorca's poem "Romance Sonámbulo," which repeats the line "Verde que
 te quiero verde," or "Green, how I want you green," throughout.

PAN

Mention of "the dead" in reference to what is stored in a pithos is influenced
 by Giorgos Vavouranakis, "Funerary Pithoi in Bronze Age Crete: Their
 Introduction and Significance at the Threshold of Minoan Palatial
 Society," *American Journal of Archaeology* 118, no. 2 (2014): 197–222.

PRE-MEMORY

"Postmemory han is a paradox": Seo-Young Chu, "Science Fiction and
 Postmemory Han in Contemporary Korean American Literature,"
 MELUS 33, no. 4 (2008): 97–121.

WHO WE GONNA CALL

The title "Who We Gonna Call" is a reference to the original "Ghost-
 busters" theme song, to the film of the same name, by Ray Parker Jr.

VALE OF THE SHADOW OF DEATH or EXTRA! EXTRA! READ ALL ABOUT IT!

The line "a slur is a sound that beasts us" is inspired by lines in Lucille Clifton's seven-part poem "far memory," in part six, "karma," which reads "the broken vows / hang against your breasts, / each bead a word / that beats you."

CONDOLENCE

Cecilia was a sixteen-year-old Yakama tribal member from Toppenish, Washington, who died of the flu at the Chemawa Indian School, a US government–run boarding institution in Salem, Oregon. This poem "erases" a letter of condolence from the superintendent of the Yakama Indian Agency to Cecilia's mother, Grace Nye. Cecilia was one of thousands of Native Americans who perished from the flu epidemic. It was a devastating blow for the Indigenous population on the heels of near-annihilation from genocide, abject poverty, disenfranchisement, disease, and brutal forced relocation.

The head nurse Daisy Codding recorded a staggering 150 flu cases and thirteen deaths at the school. As the superintendent writes: "I was so extremely busy that it was impossible for me to tell you the particulars in connection with the death of Cecilia." Cecilia died more than two hundred miles from her family, which was no rarity among Indigenous children. Under the creed "Kill the Indian in him, and save the man," the US government removed tens of thousands of Native American children from their families and forced them into federally run boarding schools for assimilation. As Cecilia's death shows, genocidal education could indeed "kill the Indian." The superintendent's letter ends: "Trusting that Cecilia's body reached you in good shape and sympathizing with you, I am." The Chemawa Indian School remains the oldest boarding school for Native American students still operating in the country.

Dana Hedgpeth, "Native American Tribes Were Already Being Wiped
Out—Then the 1918 Flu Hit," *Washington Post*, September 27, 2020,
https://www.washingtonpost.com/history/2020/09/28/1918-flu
-native-americans-coronavirus.

"Members of Oregon's Congressional Delegation Continue to Demand
Answers Surrounding Chemawa Indian School," Congressional
Documents and Publications, Federal Information & News Dispatch,
LLC, 2018.

SELMA EPP

Catherine Arnold, *Pandemic 1918: Eyewitness Accounts from the Greatest
Medical Holocaust in Modern History* (New York: St. Martin's Press,
2018), 124.

THE DONOHUE FAMILY

Arnold, *Pandemic 1918*, 126.

DONOHUE FAMILY LEDGERS

Arnold, *Pandemic 1918*, 126–127.

DC PUTSCH

The title "DC Putsch" is a reference to the Beer Hall Putsch, or Munich
Putsch, a failed coup d'état by Adolf Hitler, leader of the Nazi Party, on
November 8 and 9, 1923. After this coup, Hitler was arrested and
charged with treason.

THE SOLDIERS (OR PLUMMER)

During the First World War, the US Army was still racially segregated.
Most African American service personnel were placed in noncombative

roles, separate from whites. Over 100 Black physicians served as US Army Medical Corps officers, along with 12 Black dental officers, 639 Black infantry officers, and 400,000 Black enlisted men. Fourteen Black women served as navy clerks. Discriminatory administrative barriers prevented trained African American nurses from joining the war effort, but the public health crisis of the 1918 epidemic finally allowed eighteen Black nurses to be the first of their race ever to serve in the Army Nurse Corp during the epidemic and the war's aftermath.

"Roy Underwood Plummer": "Cpl. Roy Underwood Plummer's World War I Diary," Smithsonian, National Museum of African American History and Culture, last modified June 17, 2021, https://transcription .si.edu/project/26177.

"dutifully kept a diary": Douglas Remley, "In Their Own Words: Diaries and Letters by African American Soldiers," National Museum of African American History and Culture, last modified May 18, 2020, https://nmaahc.si.edu/explore/stories/collection/in-their-own-words.

"Most African American service personnel": "African Americans in the Military during World War I," National Archives, last modified August 28, 2020, https://research.wou.edu/c.php?g=551307&p=3785490.

"finally allowed eighteen Black nurses": Marian Moser Jones and Matilda Saines, "The Eighteenth of 1918–1919: Black Nurses and the Great Flu Pandemic in the United States," *American Journal of Public Health* 106, no. 6 (June 2019): 878.

WAR: WHAT, IS IT GOOD?

The title "War: What, Is It Good?" is a play on the song "War" by Edwin Starr, from the 1970 album *War & Peace*.

"The 1918 influenza killed": Kenneth C. Davis, *More Deadly Than War: The Hidden History of the Spanish Flu and the First World War* (New York: Henry Holt and Co., 2018).

"the British pioneered cable cutting": Gordon Corera, "How Britain

Pioneered Cable-Cutting in World War One," *BBC News*, December
15, 2017, https://www.bbc.com/news/world-europe-42367551.

"refusing to print doctors' letters": Becky Little, "As the 1918 Flu Emerged,
Cover-Up and Denial Helped It Spread," History, last modified May 26,
2020, history.com/news/1918-pandemic-spanish-flu-censorship.

"The British Army Postal Service delivered": "Letters to Loved Ones,"
Imperial War Museums, last modified December 14, 2020,
https://www.iwm.org.uk/history/letters-to-loved-ones.

"General Orders No. 48": "Soldiers' Mail," The National WWI Museum
and Memorial, last modified July 8, 2021, https://www.theworldwar
.org/learn/wwi/post-office.

"reported its post office": "Archive Record," The National WWI Museum
and Memorial, last modified September 1, 2021, https://theworldwar
.pastperfectonline.com/archive/A346097B-03F6-49BE
-A749-422059799862.

"condolence cards sold out in 2020": Michael Corkery and Sapna
Maheshwari, "Sympathy Cards Are Selling Out," *New York Times,* April
28, 2020, https://www.nytimes.com/2020/04/27/business
/coronavirus-sympathy-cards.html.

"a majority of United States": "USPS Market Research and Insights:
COVID Mail Attitudes—Understanding & Impact (April 2020),"
United States Postal Service, last modified May 1, 2020,
https://postalpro.usps.com/market-research/covid-mail-attitudes.

The line "What place have we in our histories except the present" is
influenced by D. H. Lawrence's poem "Under the Oak," specifically the
final line, "What place have you in my histories?"

THE FELLOWSHIP

"Letter from Ida B. Wells-Barnett to President Woodrow Wilson,"
DocsTeach, last modified September 19, 2021, https://www.docsteach
.org/documents/document/ida-b-wells-wilson.

TEXT TILES: THE NAMES

"The Names": Joe Brown, A Promise to Remember: The Names Project Book of Letters, Remembrances of Love from the Contributors to the Quilt (New York: Avon Books, 1992).

"27.2 to 47.8 million people": "Global HIV & AIDS Statistics — Fact Sheet," UNAIDS, last modified July 1, 2020, https://www.unaids.org /en/resources/fact-sheet.

National AIDS Memorial, last modified December 14, 2020, https://www.aidsmemorial.org/.

REPORT ON MIGRATION OF ROES

"Red Summer": July can be hot as hate. But we know this better than anyone. The "Red Summer" of 1919, as well as the immediate years surrounding it, were arguably the worst period of white-on-Black violence ever seen in the United States. From 1917 through 1923, at least a thousand Americans were killed in racial clashes across the country. The bloodshed occurred at the collision of already high-running racial tensions. African Americans, during what is called the Great Migration, left the rural South seeking opportunities in Northern cities. With the end of World War I, white veterans returned home, viewing Black laborers as competition for jobs. Meanwhile, Black servicemen returned from fighting for democracy overseas only to be denied basic civil rights at home. Additionally, the country, particularly its more densely populated areas, was still reeling from the third wave of the deadly 1918 influenza, and whites frequently blamed African Americans for the spread of the illness.

With all these roiling stressors, the Ku Klux Klan resurged, and at least sixty-four lynchings of African Americans occurred in 1918. During the escalating bloodshed from the summer of 1919, at least twenty-five racial riots erupted all over the nation. Hundreds of African American men, women, and children were burned alive, lynched, dragged, shot, stoned, hanged, or beaten to death by roving white mobs. Thousands of homes and businesses burned to the ground, leaving Black families homeless and jobless. While white assailants faced no punishment, Black Americans (many innocent) were tried and convicted by all-white juries.

The nation's capital wasn't spared the stain of racial terror. At least 39 people died and 150 were injured over a four-day period of violence in late July. Eventually two thousand federal troops were deployed (ironically, many of the white attackers were white military members freshly returned to the capital after WWI).

1919's season of strife was dubbed "Red Summer" by the NAACP's first Black executive field secretary James Weldon Johnson (author of "Lift Every Voice and Sing," also known as "the Black national anthem"). Johnson wrote about seeing DC in the NAACP's *The Crisis* magazine. "If We Must Die" by Claude McKay, a sonnet, became the Red Summer anthem. Despite the hundreds of deaths it caused, there is still no national commemorative remembrance for the Red Summer (or for the 1918 influenza). See sources below. For a poetry book on the 1919 Chicago riots, see: Eve L. Ewing, *1919* (Chicago: Haymarket Books, 2019).

"1917 through 1923": William M. Tuttle, *Race Riot: Chicago in the Red Summer of 1919* (Urbana: University of Illinois Press, 1996).

"sixty-four lynchings": "The Red Summer of 1919," History, last modified August 6, 2020, https://history.com/topics/black-history/chicago-race -riot-of-1919.

_ _ _ _ _ [GATED]

The line "Ha, we're so pained, / We probably thought / That poem was about us" is influenced by the song "You're So Vain" by Carly Simon.

The lines "Anyone who has lived / Is an historian & an artifact" are influenced by Anne Carson's poetry book *Nox*, specifically the line "One who asks about things . . . is an historian."

Courtney Coughenour et al., "Estimated Car Cost as a Predictor of Driver Yielding Behaviors for Pedestrians," *Journal of Transport & Health* 16 (February 2020): 100831, https://doi.org/10.1016/j.jth.2020.100831.

Natassia Mattoon et al., "Sidewalk Chicken: Social Status and Pedestrian Behavior," California State University, Long Beach, last modified July 22, 2021, https://homeweb.csulb.edu/~nmattoon/sidewalkposter.pdf.

Nicholas H. Wolfinger, "Passing Moments: Some Social Dynamics of Pedestrian Interaction," *Journal of Contemporary Ethnography* 24, no. 3 (October 1995): 323–340, https://doi.org/10.1177/089124195024003004.

FURY & FAITH

I'm grateful for Kira Kleaveland and the whole *CBS This Morning* team for first giving a home to the poems "Fury & Faith" and "The Miracle of Morning," among others.

THE TRUTH IN ONE NATION

The title and refrain "The Truth in One Nation" is inspired by the quote "The truth is one nation, under drugs, under drones," from Ocean Vuong's book *On Earth We're Briefly Gorgeous.*

"war has changed": Yasmeen Abutaleb et al., "'The War Has Changed': Internal CDC Document Urges New Messaging, Warns Delta Infections Likely More Severe," *Washington Post,* July 29, 2021, https://washingtonpost.com/health/2021/07/29/cdc-mask-guidance.

The line "Silence least of all" is inspired by the book *Your Silence Will Not Protect You* by Audre Lorde.

LIBATIONS

The poem "Libations" takes on a shape inspired by that of Layli Long Soldier's poem "Obligations 2."

MONOMYTH

Timeline sources:

Ben Casselman and Patricia Cohen, "A Widening Toll on Jobs: 'This Thing Is Going to Come for Us All,'" *New York Times*, April 2, 2021, https://www.nytimes.com/2020/04/02/business/economy/coronavirus-unemployment-claims.html.

Clint Smith, *How the Word Is Passed: A Reckoning with the History of Slavery Across America* (New York: Little, Brown and Company, 2021).

Derrick Bryson Taylor, "A Timeline of the Coronavirus Pandemic," *New York Times*, March 17, 2021, http://www.nytimes.com/article/coronavirus-timeline.html.

Drew Kann, "Extreme Drought and Deforestation Are Priming the Amazon Rainforest for a Terrible Fire Season," CNN, June 22, 2021, https://cnn.com/2021/06/22/weather/brazil-drought-amazon-rainforest-fires/index.html.

Eddie Burkhalter et al., "Incarcerated and Infected: How the Virus Tore Through the U.S. Prison System," *New York Times*, April 10, 2021, https://www.nytimes.com/interactive/2021/04/10/us/covid-prison-outbreak.html.

Josh Holder, "Tracking Coronavirus Vaccinations Around the World," *New York Times*, September 19, 2021, https://www.nytimes.com/interactive/2021/world/covid-vaccinations-tracker.html.

Kathy Katella, "Our Pandemic Year—A COVID-19 Timeline," Yale Medicine, last modified March 9, 2021, https://www.yalemedicine.org/news/covid-timeline.

"Listings of WHO's Response to Covid-19," World Health Organization, last modified January 29, 2021, https://www.who.int/news/item/29-06-2020-covidtimeline.

Thomas Fuller, John Eligon, and Jenny Gross, "Cruise Ship, Floating Symbol of America's Fear of Coronavirus, Docks in Oakland," *New York Times*, March 9, 2020, https://www.nytimes.com/2020/03/09/us/coronavirus-cruise-ship-oakland-grand-princess.html.

"A Timeline of COVID-19 Vaccine Developments in 2021," AJMC, last modified June 3, 2021, https://www.ajmc.com/view/a-timeline-of-covid-19-vaccine-developments-in-2021.

The Visual and Data Journalism Team, "California and Oregon 2020 Wildfires in Maps, Graphics and Images," *BBC News*, September 18, 2020, https://www.bbc.com/news/world-us-canada-54180049.

THE HILL WE CLIMB

The line "History has its eyes on us" is a reference to "History Has Its Eyes on You" from *Hamilton*.

PERMISSIONS:

Cameron Awkward-Rich. Excerpt from "Essay on the Appearance of Ghosts." Copyright © 2016, Cameron Awkward-Rich.

Dustin Lance Black, quote from Academy Originals Creative Spark Series (2014). Used by permission.

Anne Carson, from *NOX*, copyright © 2010 by Anne Carson. Reprinted by permission of New Directions Publishing Corp.

Don Mee Choi. Quote from *DMZ Colony*, copyright © 2020 by Don Mee Choi. Used with permission of the author and Wave Books.

Lucille Clifton, excerpt from "far memory 7: gloria mundi" from *The Book of Light*. Copyright © 1993 by Lucille Clifton. Reprinted with the permission of The Permissions Company, LLC, on behalf of Copper Canyon Press, coppercanyonpress.org.

Lin-Manuel Miranda. Excerpt from the composition "Take a Break," from the Broadway musical *Hamilton*. Music and lyrics by Lin-Manuel Miranda. Copyright © 2015 5000 Broadway Music (ASCAP). All rights reserved. Used by permission.

M. NourbeSe Philip, excerpt from "Notanda," from the book *Zong!* Copyright © 2008, published by Wesleyan University Press, Middletown, Connecticut. Used by permission.

Tracy K. Smith, excerpt from "Ghazal," from *Wade in the Water*. Copyright © 2018 by Tracy K. Smith. Reprinted with the permission of The Permissions Company, LLC, on behalf of Graywolf Press, Minneapolis, Minnesota, graywolfpress.org.

GRATITUDE

Thank you for being willing to carry these words with you.

It wasn't easy to write, and I'm sure it wasn't easy to read. For your getting here, I salute you.

While penning this book, I often felt lost at sea. All my thanks, in no particular order, to those who have kept me afloat until I reached the shore.

This book was written in Los Angeles, which is Tongva land. I want to thank the original keepers of this beautiful place I call home.

I'm exceptionally grateful for my selfless and tireless agent, Steve Malk, whom I consider not only a close friend but family. Thank you for constantly believing in me and the meaning of this book, even when I was bone-tired and doubtful.

All my thanks to my editor, Tamar Brazis, who was so gentle and generous in helping me bring my full vision of this work to life. I'd like to give huge applause to my Penguin Random House team, including but not limited to Markus Dohle, Madeline McIntosh, Jen Loja, Ken Wright, Felicia Frazier, Shanta Newlin, Emily Romero, Carmela Iaria, Krista Ahlberg, Marinda Valenti, Sola Akinlana, Abigail Powers, Meriam Metoui, Jim Hoover, Opal Roengchai, Grace Han, and Deborah Kaplan.

To my English teachers throughout my education, who helped hold and hone my love of literature—Shelly Fredman (who first made me realize I wanted to be a writer), Alexandra Padilla and Sara Hammerman (who magnanimously shepherded me through that torturous patch that is high school), Laura van den Berg (who taught me to write to my ghosts and not run from them), Christopher Spaide (who taught me contemporary poetry with both a keen and kind eye), and Leah Whittington and Daniel Blank (who helped me fall in love with the classics and Shakespeare). I'm also indebted to other teachers—Eric Cleveland, Pop, for supporting my fascination with biology and for your weekly fatherly texts to make sure I was still alive and actually eating while knee-deep in writing this thing; Bart Barnokowski, for rigorously introducing me to the cultural sociology that I depend on in my work; Álvaro Lopez Fernandez, Marta Olivas, the team at *Temblor*, IES Madrid, and my Spanish host family (hola, Pilar y Marucha!), who so lovingly tended to my learning of the Spanish language. I promise I still remember, um … some of it.

To my Weekly Writer Support Group, Taylor and Najya—where would I be without our Saturday morning FaceTime check-ins? (The answer is "not done with this book.") Thank you for being my cheerleaders with pens for pom-poms. To my cousin Maya for sending me funny videos when I need them and always making me laugh.

To Tara Kole and Danny Passman, my lawyer parents, who are my two last remaining brain cells on any given day, thank you for so fervently believing in my journey from the very first day we met. I cherish you both dearly.

To Caroline Sun, my book publicist, and Laura Hatanaka, my assistant, you are the indomitable mother hens who always put my time, sanity, and creativity first (even if I mostly use that time to mindlessly send you *Star Trek* GIFs—hee hee), as well as to Courtney Longshore for her tireless support behind the scenes.

A big hug for their incredible encouragement to Sylvie Rabineau, Michelle Bohan, Romola Ratnam, Pierre Elliott, Brandon Shaw (AKA BS), and Carmine Spena. Queen-worthy claps to my fierce and fabulous press gladiators, Vanessa Anderson and Erin Patterson, as well as the entire AM PR Group.

I am also indebted to my high school writing mentors: Michelle Chahine and Dinah Berland from the nonprofit WriteGirl, who spent Wednesday afternoons writing with me at loud tea shops while I messily munched on crumbly coffee cake, and India Radfar, who mentored me at Beyond Baroque. Thanks to Jamie Frost, my former speech therapist, as well as my spiritual-doppelganger mentor, Blessing.

A huge shout-out to Urban Word, a program that supports youth poets laureate in more than sixty cities, regions, and states nationally, which has given me the incredible honor of serving as a youth poet laureate several times in my life. Thank you to Vital Voices, who funded my community literacy project One Pen One Page, and to the ongoing support of Nicco Melle and Mass Poetry as well as Jen Benka and the Academy of American Poets.

I'm deeply appreciative of my fellow poets for their support: Tracy K. Smith, who has been a fairy god-poet to me ever since we shared the stage at the Library of Congress; Richard Blanco, who is always a phone call away and willing to speak with me in Spanish just so I can practice; Elizabeth Alexander, who called immediately when I was named the 2020 inaugural poet and gave me spiritual soul food over the phone. I'm also thankful for the poetry magic of Jacqueline Woodson, Eve Ewing, Clint Smith, Luis Rodriguez, and Juan Felipe Herrera, whose work inspires me perennially.

To Lin-Manuel Miranda, who years ago let my speechless self tuck a poem into his hand. To Malala, your friendship means so much to this girl. To Oprah, your mentorship, guidance, and luminosity is such a privilege.

Dr. Merije, I know you had to visit me tooooo many times because I'd run myself sick and ragged working on this. But you always did it with a joke, which made the sniffles worth it.

We're almost to the end, folks! To my Girl Gang, Alex, Haley, and Bib, thanks for dealing with my moans about this book over group chat.

Above all, I'm deeply indebted to my family: my fierce, fabulous, and formidable mom, who made me everything I am today; my talented twin and ride-or-die partner in crime since diapers, Gabrielle (GG); my grandmothers, for persistently making sure I'm eating, sleeping, and taking my vitamins; and the fluffy pooch Lulu, who sits beside me whenever I'm struggling to finish a poem. I love you all with every beating of my heart.

Thank you to God. Thank you, my ancestors.

I am the daughter of Black writers. I am descended from freedom fighters who broke their chains and changed the world. They call me. I carry them always.

Love,

Amanda

AMANDA GORMAN

is the youngest presidential inaugural poet in US history. She is a committed advocate for the environment, racial equality, and gender justice. In 2017, Urban Word named her the first-ever National Youth Poet Laureate. Gorman's performance of her poem "The Hill We Climb" at the 2021 Presidential Inauguration received critical acclaim and international attention. The special edition of her inaugural poem debuted at #1 on the *New York Times*, *USA Today*, and *Wall Street Journal* bestseller lists. She is also the author of the children's picture book *Change Sings*. After graduating cum laude from Harvard University, she now lives in her hometown of Los Angeles.